Sex, Status & Sticky Toffee Pudding

The Secrets to Becoming a Successful Entrepreneur

Chris Hill

Sex, Status & Sticky Toffee Pudding
The Secrets to Becoming a
Successful Entrepreneur
©2024 Christopher John Hill

ISBN: 9781068529306 Paperback

Published by: Inspired By Publishing

The strategies in this book are presented primarily for enjoyment and educational purposes. Every effort has been made to trace copyright holders and obtain their permission for the use of copyright material.

The information and resources provided in this book are based upon the authors' personal experiences. Any outcome, income statements or other results, are based on the authors' experiences and there is no guarantee that your experience will be the same. There is an inherent risk in any business enterprise or activity and there is no guarantee that you will have similar results as the author as a result of reading this book.

The author reserves the right to make changes and assumes no responsibility or liability whatsoever on behalf of any purchaser or reader of these materials.

DEDICATION

This book is dedicated to anyone out there who has the want, the energy and the tenacity to get more from life but has yet to find that path to success. You can, you will and you *deserve* all the success in the world. Follow the steps in this book, become obsessed with the outcome and remember to have a few sticky toffee puddings on your travels.

ACKNOWLEDGEMENTS

To write this book, I have travelled through a lifetime of experiences that have both shaped my perspective in life and brought me untold happiness and success. I would like to thank those closest to me for everything they have done along my journey and for the support I know they will continue to provide in the future.

Staying consistent with my value of family first, I'd like to begin by thanking my parents (both biological and not). You have all brought different elements to my upbringing and I love and cherish all of you more than you can know. Thank you.

To my brother – we are peas in the same pod and together we could take on anything. I love and look up to you, and here's to the next chapters in our lives as we take on new challenges that each of us has already conquered. Thank you.

And of course, to my beautiful wife and incredible children – you are my reason for being, the light in my life and everything that makes my world special. I feel incredibly blessed to have you by my side. You keep me humble, keep me silly and keep me inspired to achieve more while savouring every moment we share. Without you I wouldn't be able to accomplish what I do, nor would I have the same desire to. Thank you.

Professionally, I'd like to thank these mentors, without whom I likely wouldn't have found this path to success or achieved it so quickly and effectively.

Angie, you showed me I could be more than I ever dreamed, and all I had to do was shift my perspective. You made me believe it was possible and that I deserved it. Thank you.

Christian, in a very short time, you reshaped my perspective on strategy and business and taught me a new level of the synergy between brand and customer experience – all while having a great time and building a strong friendship. Thank you.

And finally, my business partner, friend and brother from another mother Kunal Dattani, without whom this journey would be nowhere near as enjoyable or purposeful. It's been a hell of a ride to date, and the future only holds greater things for us. I'm grateful for everything you have brought and continue to bring to the party. Thank you.

CONTENTS

INTRODUCTION

Success is reserved for the elite few who are born with a gift. You will *never* be able to achieve their level of success.

Only one of these statements is true.

If you are reading this book, I want to congratulate you for taking the first step to becoming one of the 2% of people who will actually realise success. Yes, you read that right. About 98% of people who walk this earth will die having never achieved their goals and dreams, which means success is an elusive creature that only a few get to gaze upon and enjoy.

So what does it take to become successful and how can you ensure you avoid becoming one of the 98%? That is what this book is going to deliver, a practical guide that will empower you to create your very own path to success.

Tucked away in the pages of this book are the strategies and blueprints for building that path. These have been forged throughout my lifetime and condensed into a simple, step-by-step guide. If you apply these principles to your life with the same honesty and grit they were written with, they will bring you untold amounts of success, time and time again. You will be able to replicate this success over and over again, even as your goalposts shift and adapt for you to achieve things that, up until now, might have only seemed possible in a dream.

Sounds simple doesn't it? So, if it's as easy as following a guide to reach success, then why are 98% of people living their entire lives without it?

To answer that, we first need to understand what success actually means:

> **Success, n.** The accomplishment of an aim or purpose.

The difficulty with success is that under this description, it would be very easy for all to accomplish it. You could set yourself a simple task you know you can do, such as "clap your hands three times" or "say your name aloud," and as soon as the action was complete you would be successful. However, these are not the successes we are chasing in this book.

When I talk about success, what I really mean is for you to achieve your biggest life goals, to overcome your greatest fears, to realise the outcome of your full potential, to dream big and to achieve *bigger*.

Now, if I were to ask you to write just one sentence on a piece of paper about what that looks like for you, would you be able to? Could you commit to that one statement and destination, and be 100% happy with the success when you arrive at the finish line?

I believe that there are only a few people who are born with that foresight, the ability to know exactly what they were put on earth to achieve and the energy and passion to chase it from day one. Some people call this a divine purpose or a soul purpose, and if you have this built into you, it is a gift that you should be eternally grateful for.

However, for the vast majority of us, we learn our purpose on the journey, by trying and testing different elements that surround us until we hone in on a handful of things that we want to achieve. Success changes as we walk this path, and for each of us the journey and destination will look different. But, there will always be commonalities in the characteristics of how success manifests itself.

In this book, we are going to delve into those characteristics, so that as you choose and test your paths to success you can always keep a measure and balance. This will not only speed up your journey but also make it more fulfilling.

I will be taking you through 13 steps to get you from where you are now to where you want to go. Even if you can't clearly see where that is yet, by the end of this book you will understand your destination and the path to get there.

To achieve that, we will be covering all aspects of your success journey. Below is a glimpse of what we will cover as you work your way through this book.

Understanding

To be successful, we first need to understand what success really means to us, so that when we get there, we are not disappointed. Using tools like the Health, Wealth and Happiness Triangle while delving into the topics of sex and status, you will be able to get a clearer picture of the things that make up your version of success.

Beliefs

When we understand what we are trying to achieve, the next hurdle that comes into view is one of the hardest to overcome – our own self-imposed obstacles. One of the most counterproductive human traits is creating blockades and hurdles in our path that we can never seem to leap over, no matter how hard we try. In later chapters, we will not only discover the origins of these hurdles but also remove them altogether – instead of trying to jump over them.

Preparation

The more prep we put into something before we begin, the more likely we will achieve the goal and enjoy the journey. Success is no different. By plotting our route in our Personal Success Sat-Nav and preparing for the trials and tribulations the route will give us – from everyday obstacles to unexpected moments, like planning a funeral – you will be prepared for whatever the world throws at you, keeping your feet firmly placed on the path to success.

Support and Celebrations

Every journey is easier with support. Even with all the prep in place, having a guide who has trodden your chosen path is always worthwhile. As you embark on your journey, I will share how to find these guides and mentors; and when they help you reach the peaks of success, I'll show you how to recognise and celebrate the feats you have accomplished.

If you follow the steps and guidelines in this book, not only will you find your own success, but you will also be able to achieve it without trying to replicate the "gurus" and that "one thing" they did religiously to reach success. You won't need to get up at 5am, meditate, become a traveller of the world or a ton of other things that others claim to be the key to success. Instead, you will be able to create your own path and journey by understanding what the keys to *your* success are. And you'll understand how to discover these keys, use them and change them as time goes on.

This is the reason I chose to write this book in the first place. When I started my journey, there wasn't a guide I could pick up and apply to my life that would genuinely help me understand and achieve my own success. Instead, I had to do hours of research, make all the mistakes on the way to the top and feel the pains that they brought along with them.

When I started shooting for success, I was just putting endless hours into chasing money, selling time for cash. I knew I could be more, but I had those hurdles deeply rooted in my internal beliefs – and for good reason. I left school with limited education, no prospects or dreams, and a world that was screaming at me to become employed and just be "the best I can be" each day. It took me decades of work, trial and error, self-discovery and more to remove my self-limiting beliefs and realise I could be more – that I could challenge perceptions and build an empire of 6- and 7-figure businesses, all from the ground up.

If you are anything like I was, you likely have a bookshelf full of self-help books. After each one, you get a boost of energy and a new guru-style approach to try, believing it would be the next thing to get you to the top. The reality is, you probably tried, got bored and moved on to the next book, leaving behind an impressive bookcase of things you implemented in your life for a short period but that didn't really get you where you needed to be.

I'm not giving you another one of those books. Instead, I am condensing everything I have learned, every book I have read, every conversation I have had into this one guide so you don't have to spend years chasing and learning. With this book, you can take the shortcut to your best health, your most intense happiness, untold wealth and overall success with as little resistance as possible.

Although this book is going to unlock these things for you, there is one thing you *must* do to take full advantage of what I will share with you in the following chapters. It is the one thing that neither I nor anyone else can help you with, yet it is fundamental to successfully implementing the contents of this book: your own desire and urgency in taking action. It might seem like you have plenty of time to achieve your goals, but time is an uncontrollable variable, and we all have an unseen countdown running with no way of knowing how much time remains.

It might be decades, years, months or days, and our current age or health is not enough of a measure to go by when trying to estimate exactly what we have in the tank. Time can be your biggest friend or your most feared enemy, and unfortunately it can switch between the two at a moment's notice. So, if you want to start chasing success and take advantage of the opportunities you have ahead, the journey needs to start today, and you need to put more energy into this path than you have ever put into any task before.

The journey can be tough at times, it can be frustrating and feel like an uphill battle, but trust me when I say that the juice is worth the squeeze. With the shortcuts you will learn in this book, success can be closer than you think – as long as you approach it with the right mindset and urgency.

That ability to create urgency around any task is a super power that's common amongst the elite who find success. It took me a long time to realise this, but that urgency to start a task or try something to see if it works is key when you want to become part of the 2%. Even if you've been failing in your attempts, trying brings you closer to success because you learn what doesn't work, rather than being stuck wondering what might have happened if you hadn't tried at all.

Failure is going to be part of this success, and although it can be disheartening, it will eventually become just another stitch on your tapestry. Any failure will eventually seem insignificant in the face of successes that come soon afterwards.

So, which of the statements I said at the beginning of the chapter is true?

> Success is reserved for the elite few who are born with a gift.

> You will *never* be able to achieve their level of success.

It might surprise you to learn that it's actually the second statement, and here is why:

Success is not reserved for the elite who are born with a gift. I believe anyone can achieve success as long as they have the commitment to being consistent and tenacious with their journey. You will learn in the chapters of this book that I am a walking example of how anyone can become successful, regardless of their ability and start in life. So, if success is open to all, why won't you achieve the success that the "elite" already have?

Put simply, the reason you will not experience their level of success is because that success is individual to them. Success is a personal and individual target with no two people's version of it looking the same, like a fingerprint or the stripes on a zebra's back. At a glance, they might look the same, but as you zoom in and explore each line and pattern, there are fundamental differences that belong only to that person, whether it be in the way the success was achieved or how and why it means so much to them.

Your journey to mapping out that success starts now. By the end of this book, you will have a clear understanding of how it looks to you and the practical steps to make it your new reality.

CHAPTER 1
THE HEALTH, WEALTH AND HAPPINESS TRIANGLE

If you were to ask my parents what I was like as a young child growing up, they would probably describe my defining characteristics as considerate, kind, funny and caring. The terms "old before his time" and "an old head on young shoulders" were often bandied around when "adults" spoke about me. To be fair, they were pretty accurate. I was the second and last child in our family unit, born 18 months after my brother who, in those 18 months, had done everything in his power to put my parents off having more children!

So, when I came into the world with the ability to blend into the background of the existing chaos, moving through the day with little fuss or need, it was a welcome relief to a set of tired and overworked parents who were getting to grips with our ever-evolving family unit. My mum has recounted on many occasions that, for the first year of my life, I was referred to as "baby" rather than my name, simply because it was easier to talk about me in that context to my brother. Everything was just so fast-paced with two kids under two years old in the house. "Baby needs to sleep, so be calmer," or "It's baby's lunchtime, so you need to have yours, too," are phrases my mom would frequently tell my brother.

As the years went by, the same dynamic continued in our family, with my brother usually residing comfortably in the centre of attention, basking in the spotlight that he would create, and me on the sidelines looking in, observing from the gallery where I could get a more holistic view of the moment as it unfolded around me.

While writing these first few paragraphs, I am aware they could be read in many different ways, with the chance of being misinterpreted as negative reflections of my upbringing. Please let me clarify this is far from the case. These were, in fact, very happy times for me. In future chapters, I will delve deeper into how parts of our upbringing create what I refer to as our biggest "superpowers," and for me, these moments formed one of them.

Without the need to grow up in the spotlight, from a very young age, I could observe from afar how people interacted with one another, picking up on small details that would usually go missed or unnoticed. This included observing how emotional connections were formed and maintained, as well as how the atmosphere in a room could change during different events and moments.

Over time I pieced together the communication puzzle, pulling together the similarities and nuances of each interaction, until it became a hidden sixth sense of mine. I could tune into this sixth sense, giving me the ability to understand and engage in conversations with people of all ages and backgrounds with ease, which in turn led me to *want* to engage more with people. For someone who was quite reserved as a child, that ability to communicate in comfortable surroundings made me great at personal connections. Outside of that comfort zone, it made me a better conversationalist in all walks of life. It's also contributed to my ongoing fascination with people in general – with how they move, speak and sound, and why they act the way they do.

Even now, I could waste days sitting in cafes with a fresh cup of coffee, just watching people go about their day doing every normal thing you could imagine. It fascinates me how, although we all come from different backgrounds, upbringings and situations, we can all share so many similarities in the ways we act and what we are all striving to accomplish, even amongst the clear differences between us. Even with those differences, one thing has always been very clear to me, which I believe is true for 98% of us. We all want *more*.

Whether that's more money, more success, more recognition, more love or any other "more" that you can add to this list, the human race has an insatiable appetite for growth that we all feel in one way or another. It's a fundamental need in humanity and has been a defining factor in our civilization's growth as we've adapted over millions of years, with new technologies and ways of coexisting together.

So if the majority of us have a thirst and hunger for growth to get more from life, why is it that only the top 2% of us achieve the heights of success that we all crave? Why is it that some people have the ability to not only dream big, but to crystalise those dreams into reality? Are the successful amongst us all following the same tried and tested blueprint that is only available to the ultra-elite? Or perhaps these people are all built and raised in a certain way, predestined for great things?

The truth? No, the ultra-successful are not all following the same path, the same rules or the same blueprints. They all come from different backgrounds and different levels of wealth; some from loving homes and some from broken ones; some are highly educated and some dropped out of school; some are extroverted and some are heavily introverted. So how is it possible that they all still manage to become successful, while 98% of the population will never know the levels of success that they do? What is the secret to their success?

I believe it's because they were able to truly understand who they are, how they best work and what it means to *them* to be successful. They have not tried to achieve their goals by following someone else's methods of success. Instead, they have taken inspiration from the world around them and figured out how they could best apply it to their own ways of working. Successful people have created a path they can walk with ease, building on their skill sets daily and adapting to new ways of succeeding when the landscape around them changes. Instead of relying on a single method, tool or system fixed in their routine, they understand that success comes from adapting and evolving.

Take a second to think about the results you might get by copying the exact methods of someone else to achieve your goals. Let's imagine your goal was to be able to show more unconditional love for your family, even when they act out of turn or behave in a way you would not find favourable. You look to the world around you for inspiration and find that dogs are the most successful in giving unconditional love, and so you start to adopt their way of thinking and behaving.

How many times would you have to bark, fetch, sit on command or wait patiently at the window for your loved ones to return before you realised that this might not be the best path to your success? I would hazard a guess at not that many! While you can certainly draw inspiration from a dog's ability to show unconditional love, the specific actions a dog performs, such as barking or fetching, are unlikely to guide you on your path to success.

So what do my childhood, the top 2% and dogs have to do with the Health, Wealth and Happiness Triangle (and what is it, for that matter)? The reason I've shared this early in the book is to show that everything leading up to your reading this book has already set you on your path to success. As we delve deeper into each chapter, we are going to explore how you can build on your existing foundations to create your own clear path to success.

To understand our starting point, we first need to know where we are right now in the Health, Wealth and Happiness Triangle. This is a tool I developed and use within Lifestyle Entrepreneur to give an accurate measure of where we are in our path to achieve (or remain) successful at any given time. As a caveat to this, success is always objective to the person who is looking to achieve it. It can be made up of a number of things that can be measured, but after many rounds of testing, we found that we felt more content and successful when we had health, wealth and happiness equally balanced in abundance. When the scales started to tip away from one of these three pillars, we noticed significant changes in how we felt and how our actions were affected when the balance among these three pillars began to shift.

The Health, Wealth and Happiness Triangle

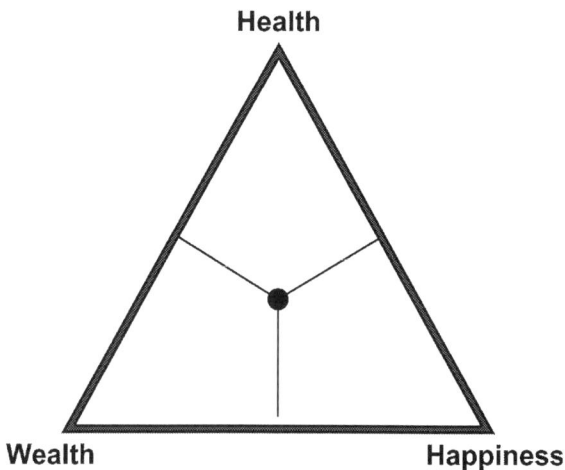

The tool is made up of an equilateral triangle with its three points being home to Health, Wealth and Happiness. All sides being equal indicate that none of the three pillars are more important than the other, and that each pillar should be treated with equal importance at all times. This is a simple yet powerful lesson for anyone reading this book, whether you're just starting out or have begun to find success in one area but still feel something is missing or different from what you expected at this stage.

Before I speak more on the three pillars, you may be asking, "Why not four or five pillars, or even more? What about the other things that remain important and that can be measured?" These are good questions and we have tested bolting on other aspects such as stress, love, cash flow, education, friendship, etc. However, we found that these ultimately contribute to either health, wealth or happiness, and for those that don't fit neatly into these categories, if they are lacking or excessive, they do not significantly impact our overall path to success.

Another thing to clarify before we dive into the balancing act of the three pillars is that it doesn't matter how vast each of them is. As an example, for wealth, you might have £10 to your name or multiple millions. The laws of the triangle remain the same and apply to all levels of success. Regardless of how far into success you travel, you *must* remain balanced in all three to feel the true force of success.

To illustrate this, I'll use the example of someone who has been chasing financial wealth for a number of years in a highly paid corporate position. They have an impressive work ethic, thinking nothing of putting in the long hours, sometimes putting in 80- to 90-hour weeks to push the business and their career forwards. Their LinkedIn profile gleams with yearly promotions and their title has the words "president" or "director" for all to see and admire. Their business success is also reflected in their monthly earnings, with a high six-figure income achieved. The most recent sports car model sits on their drive, they wear the best suits money can buy and they are highly regarded in their field. On top of that, they have invested wisely and have a portfolio of 10 rental properties exceeding £1 million in value, which they manage in the evenings and weekends, knowing it'll provide generational wealth to their family.

For all intents and purposes, they have nailed the wealth pillar, they're set for life and there isn't a huge amount that will turn the tide for them. They are "financially free." Sounds amazing doesn't it? So what did it take to get here? Let's evaluate the other two pillars.

The long hours and years of grinding haven't been too kind on their health, and in recent years, it has begun to catch up with them. Takeaways, snacking and grabbing the food they can between meetings and phone calls have led to a high salt and fat intake, with food being seen for convenience rather than fuel. Five years ago, they were diagnosed with high blood pressure, and a concoction of tablets is keeping it at bay. That said, habits have far from changed, with the hours (and pounds) still piling on each month. The echoes of "I'll start next" week are heard all too often when loved ones question their ongoing health issues. The desire to change is present, but the hunger and pull of the next level of wealth is too strong for them to ignore.

With two teenage children at home and a stay-at-home partner, their lifestyle requires constant financial input to keep up with the ever-growing demand for bigger and better possessions. Now, they almost feel as if they are in service to their family, and believe that by providing more access to money and wealth, they will be able to bring back the spark of happiness to what now feels like a cold home.

Although fictitious, the above scenario will likely resonate and crystallise as a person you know. Perhaps some of you who are reading this book might feel like you're looking into a mirror. We are driven by such deep desires, which, without clear thoughts as to *why*, can consume ourselves and our lives. This is how this person's triangle would look:

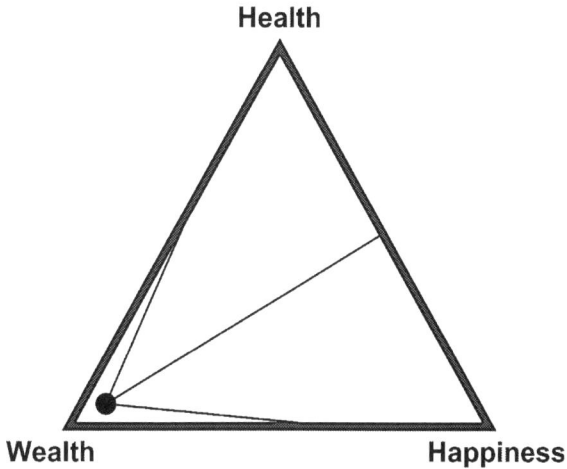

This is just one example of misbalance, and I could spend the next 50 pages giving examples of how life might look if you neglected your happiness (which we see all too often in the news, when great people are lost to the tragedy of suicide) or how, if we lack effort in the corner of health, we will likely be left with a rude awakening and a journey cut short, leaving a fantastic story without its proper conclusion.

However, there is something much more important that should fill these pages, and that's giving you proper instructions on how you can use the Health, Wealth and Happiness Triangle to either rebalance your focus or start building new foundations to success, with clear goals to accompany them. So, before we do that, we need to see the other side of the pendulum and understand how it could look and feel when everything is balanced and in perfect harmony.

When your health, wealth and happiness (which we will now refer to as HW&H for ease) balance, they will no longer need to be reviewed or considered daily, as you will simply feel at your best. It's that "spring in your step" feeling when you go about your day, with no large win or individual success inflating your satisfaction. You will feel as if in "flow," things will be easy and you will be able to cope with what the days throw at you. You will begin to "attract" good things into your life with little to no effort and your relationships will be in a good, healthy place. For the ones that do not feel that way, you will know exactly what is needed to bring them back into line and you will be content with what needs to be done to achieve it.

This is a feeling of low stress and high appreciation, resulting in great mental health and a better understanding of your emotions. This feeling can last for hours, days, months or years and is usually met with a consistent and steady progression, rather than the feeling of being stopped dead, or with the afterburners at full tilt. This is where it all feels worth it, and should be enjoyed each and every time the balance aligns.

Although this sounds like a beautiful state of being, it is not one we aim to stay in for too long as it can drive contentment and, like most budding and successful entrepreneurs, we crave growth in all areas of our lives. At Lifestyle Entrepreneur, we make a point to actively schedule these states into our year, as a way of balancing the books when we lean towards one pillar for a period of time in order to achieve more. Imagine how good it would be to schedule this feeling into your diary, as many times a year as you want!

That is what we are going to teach you in this chapter: how to understand where you are today on the triangle and how you can shift your focus to balance the books. You will also understand which pillar you have been leaning into for far too long and what you can do to refocus and balance. With this knowledge, you will then be able to actively use this method to chase the growth you are after, all while rebalancing and never risking one of the pillars ever again.

So what defines your HW&H and how can we give each of them a quantifiable score? Because without a measure of each, we will never really understand which buckets are full, and which require additional attention to bring them back into balance. Everyone's criteria will be unique to them, but we have a framework that has been designed to work for us all, which can be downloaded for free at http://www.lifestyle-entrepreneur.co.uk/stp. To illustrate how the framework works, let's begin with happiness.

To understand what makes us happy, we first need to appreciate what being happy actually means, and how it happens. The Oxford Dictionary's definition of "happy" is:

> **happy, adj. & n.** Feeling or showing a deep sense of pleasure or contentment, esp. arising from satisfaction with one's circumstances or condition

Usually, people wait for happiness to arrive, expecting it to be the end point of a project, journey or mission in which they believe the result will either make them happy or unhappy. This is a valid thought process, as happiness is often triggered by events we categorise as good or bad. It means that happiness is a choice we make daily, and the more favourable our circumstances, the happier we tend to be.

So then why are there people who are vastly "successful" and appear to have the best circumstances, yet suffer from crippling depression which sometimes ends tragically? In some cases, I believe it's because they have never understood what makes them happy in the first place.

If you ask yourself what makes you truly happy, would you know instantly? Would a list of things that make you happy include people that make you happy? Like your spouse, friends or children? Sometimes, we look to others to make us happy because we associate the feeling with them, but in reality, we are in control of our own happiness. We have to appreciate and understand what personally makes us happy. This is what the framework is for.

Now, I want you to list everything that makes you happy – but it cannot involve others influencing that happiness. I see lots of lists where people say things like "I'm just happy when everyone else is happy" which, although it is a beautiful thing, is not what creates the happy feeling in your core. So for now, focus on what *you* can do to bring happiness to yourself. There are no wrong answers here, just a list of the things that, when you do or experience them, bring happiness to you. To help, I have included an excerpt from my own list below:

Chris's Happy List

People watching with a nice cup of coffee
Walks in nature
Fine dining
Learning new recipes to cook
Reading personal development
Playing golf
Taking on new challenges

By understanding what makes you happy personally and putting them into a list, you now have the ability to choose moments that can add to your daily happiness when it is lacking. I want you to now pick the ones that you believe provide you the most happiness, and add those to the happiness pillar in our framework. Once done, I want you to put a score out of 10 against each that represents just how much of this happiness you have given yourself recently. This can then be added alongside other areas of your own happiness (like in the example below), which can include those people in your life that we omitted from our personal happy list. There can be as many columns as you like in your happiness pillar, but we choose to focus on the top three like in the example below. If you prefer, it is also okay to leave this as just one column, which means that there are other areas in your life that produce happiness. There will always be a bonus on top of your HW&H balance. Once you have filled each column in and given yourself a score for each item, it will give you an overall average score out of 10.

Personal Happiness	Score	Happiness at Home:	Score	Happiness with Friends	Score
Coffee days	10	Connected with partner	7	Golfing	2
Fine dining	5	Fun times with kids	10	Group meets	10
Cooking	8	Time with extended family	10	Staying connected	6
Average (rounded)	8	Average (rounded)	9	Average (rounded)	6
Happiness Total Average				8	

This now gives us not only the score of happiness we are feeling right now, but also the key areas we can apply focus and time to improve our overall happiness score.

We will use the total average score when we plot the results on the HW&H triangle later on, alongside the other two scores for wealth and health.

There is one caveat worth mentioning with happiness: There are events that can occur in our lives that are uncontrollable, sometimes devastating, and these sit outside of this day-to-day framework. There is something you can do to help when these moments take hold, and for that, we use Mo Gawdat's equation to happiness (from his book *Solve for Happy*), which looks like this:

Happiness = Reality / Expectation

What this means is, if your reality meets or exceeds your expectations, you will be happy. If it falls short, you will be unhappy. I once heard Mo describe this by using one event, but two expectations. The event was rain, and the two expectations for the day were sunbathing or growing new flowers in the garden.

If your expectation was to sunbathe, you are going to be disappointed/unhappy, but if you wanted to water the garden, you would be happy for the rain.

The event stays the same, but if you are able to change your expectations, you can find happiness when your original expectations are not met. Mo goes into great detail in his book on how this can be used within your life, no matter what you face, and I would highly recommend reading it if you want to learn more.

So, now that we have our average happiness score, we would do exactly the same for wealth and health, building and creating our own personal lists of what we currently hold valuable in each category. For wealth, that might be turning the tides on your finances, or building a retirement plan that gives you lifetime security.

For health, it might be losing weight, increasing cardiovascular fitness, moving more or managing an illness you have. Anything can go into these, following the same rules of creating lists you are personally in control of, and even adding external factors to them.

Make sure these lists provide a personal measure of your current situation compared to your expectations, so you have clear goals to focus on and improve your score.

With these in place, it is now time to revisit the HW&H Triangle to see how it can be used to better understand your journey to success.

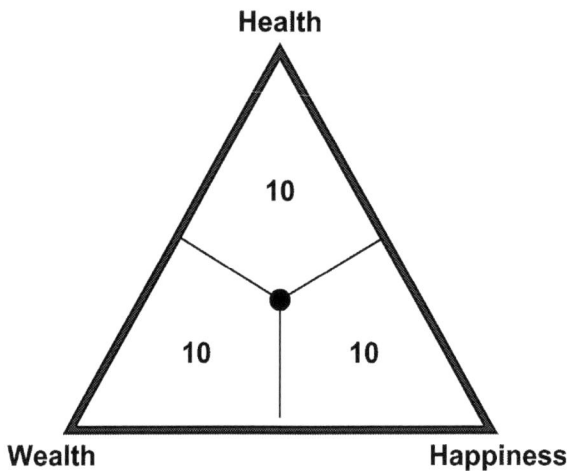

The example image I shared of the HW&H Triangle at the beginning of this chapter is a 2D version when viewed from the top and looking down. I have put this image above, now including the average score for each of the pillars.

To explain how it can be used, we need to first have a clear vision of how it would look in 3D, with us now viewing it from a side perspective. Each point of the triangle now extends upwards to a central point to form a pyramid, as seen on the next page.

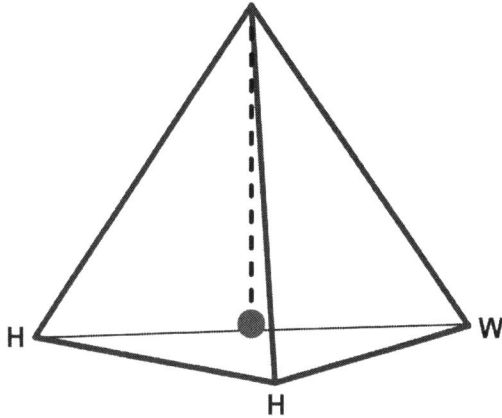

From the pyramid's point hangs a pendulum, which, when all is balanced, drops exactly into the centre of the triangle, equidistant from each of the three pillars of HW&H. Now that you have your scores, these can be added to each section, and you need to imagine that each one is pulling on the pendulum. The bigger the score, the more of a pull it has to draw the pendulum towards it. In turn, that means the lower the score, the less pull it will have, allowing the pendulum to swing away from that pillar.

Here are some examples of how this looks in reality, demonstrating how different circumstances can affect where the pendulum is pulled:

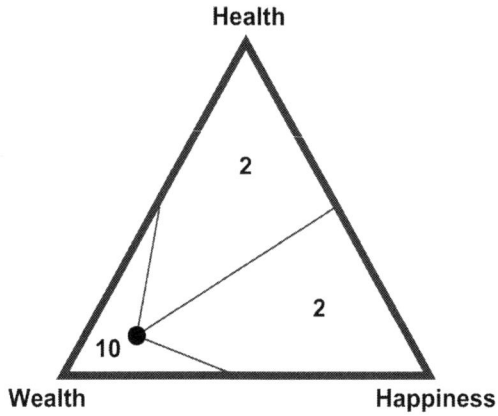

WEALTH AS A SOLE FOCUS

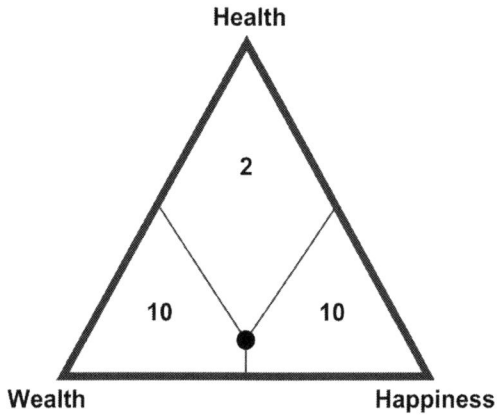

WEALTH AND HAPPINESS FOCUSED

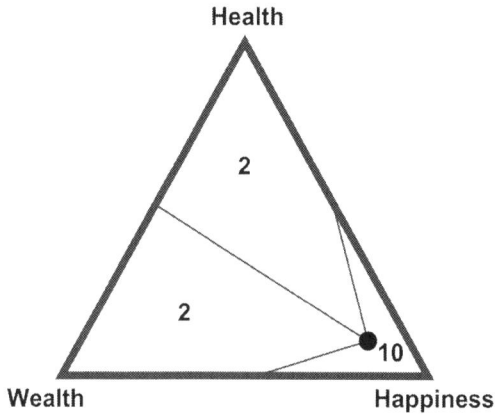

HAPPINESS AS A SOLE FOCUS

Any and all results you get from the HW&H Triangle are valid, as they will just reflect where you are putting in the most effort at any given time. Sometimes, you will be in a growth mode, where you are actively trying to grow in each or some of the areas in the triangle. This might mean leaning heavily into certain aspects or a specific pillar to give it momentum to grow, which in turn will mean other areas will suffer.

Sometimes, you will be in a phase of maintenance where you want to enjoy the balance of the three pillars, giving them all shared attention. While this does not allow for much growth, it does allow you to enjoy each section and the items that make it up.

The important thing you need to do is check in with the balance regularly, and understand how tipping the balance in any direction will cause a reaction.

The more you understand it, the more you can prepare yourself and others for how it might affect you and them.

For example, if I am going to be focusing heavily on growing our businesses, I will speak with my wife ahead of time and let her know of the pressures that will not just affect me, but will cascade to her and the children as my time is consumed elsewhere.

The same applies if more time is needed at home; I will work with my business partner to limit the damage this will have on the business and the people who work with us.

This is how we are able to schedule these times into our year, by strategically planning when we will be leaning into which pillars, to understand where we will be able to find the balance in-between.

The key to this tool is that the more you use it, and the more you involve others in it, the better you will be able to manage your levels of stress as you lean into the different levels of success.

Additionally, it prepares you and everyone involved for what might happen when your focus is pulled. It will also help you understand your tolerances in each pillar and help you avoid burnout or a progress plateau when you are pursuing your goals.

We personally use this tool every 8 to 12 weeks and have built it into our ongoing annual and general meeting agendas, where we plan our strategy in and outside of our businesses.

This enables us to stay in control of our goals with a more holistic, lifestyle-centric approach, all while keeping us accountable to our businesses, our loved ones and ourselves.

We also never lean into a pillar heavily for more than eight weeks. Even with an understanding team, family, friends and base of health, this is when you start to see the cracks appearing.

To help you manage your own Health, Wealth and Happiness Triangle, we've built an online quiz available on our website http://www.lifestyle-entrepreneur.co.uk/stp, where you can answer some simple questions to get a high-level view of where your pendulum might be sitting. The quiz will also provide you with some useful tips and tricks on how to start to restore some balance quickly and effectively.

CHAPTER 2
SEX AND STATUS

It's believed that the average human adult makes anywhere between 33,000 to 35,000 decisions every single day. Let that sink in for a minute. From the moment you open your eyes to the moment you shut them for sleep, there are up to 35,000 conscious decisions you need to make to navigate through your day. These range from small and, some might say, insignificant choices (such as which socks to wear, or how fast to run the tap while you brush your teeth) all the way up to life-changing decisions, like which house to buy, who to commit your life to or what career path you would like to take.

Some decisions are remarkably easy and almost instinctive, happening without much conscious thought, like choosing what to have for breakfast. Researchers at Cornell University estimate that we make 226.7 decisions each day on food alone! Others, however, might require hours of complex internal debate, weighing the pros and cons of each option, such as deciding which university to attend. Or, if you live in our house, the same complex internal debate applies to choosing which takeaway to get on a Friday evening!

Whatever these decisions are, if you are going to be in the driving seat of your own success, you need to make sure the majority of the decisions you make on a day-to-day basis keep you pointed in the right direction. So, how can we ensure that all 35,000 of our decisions are keeping us not only aligned to our health, wealth and happiness, but also directed towards our overall success?

I think we can all agree that if we had to sit and evaluate 35,000 decisions every single day against a method to make sure it was the correct choice, we would end up never getting anything done. The only list I have which is similar in length is my to-do list and that's not been completed in the last 36 years – and I would bet my house that I will never, ever complete it! However, it is important to understand how we might process each different type of decision so that we can start to recognise them as they happen.

There are six main decision types that come into play, and sometimes we use a number of these at once to cope with the sheer volume of decisions thrown at us daily.

1. Impulsiveness

Impulsive decisions are usually given a negative connotation, and are found in things like over-indulgence, shopping and gambling. An impulsive decision is driven by the want or need for instant gratification with little care or thought given to the long-term consequences. It can also be a decision made in haste with the first options presented to us, rather than pausing or researching all the options available in pursuit of the best possible outcome. Impulse is not to be confused with "intuition," which is a gut feeling that can be used to guide a good decision based on our existing collective knowledge of the subject or situation.

2. Reflecting and Prioritising

Reflecting and prioritising are the polar opposites of impulse. Where impulse requires little time or thought, this decision type requires the most amount of time and energy to yield the best possible decision and outcome, in the hope that it will bear the most fruit. This method best serves decisions like buying your home or choosing a university to attend (the big stuff!).

3. Delegating

Next comes delegation, which removes your need to decide for yourself by passing the responsibility to a third party or team. You are still able to retain an element of control by delegating with parameters for the decision, but ultimately it is the job of the delegate to follow through and deliver what is needed to provide the desired outcome. This might be a task such as a taxi driver picking the best route for your journey, or a loved one preparing your dinner ahead of your arrival. You might give a preference, but the end result and execution are in their hands.

4. Avoidance / Deflection

The fourth decision type is avoidance (or deflection), which might happen for a number of reasons. One could be because you are not willing to be responsible for the impact the decision might have, or it might be that you are not ready for the overwhelm that making the decision will now bring. This is more a delay tactic than an end result, and if used too much it might cause bigger issues that you wouldn't have faced if you committed to a decision earlier. An example of this might be a health problem. You avoid visiting a doctor for fear of what your ailment might be, but by deferring the decision to find out, you run the risk of greater problems or living with unjustified stress.

5. Balancing

The fifth strategy is balancing, which is essentially weighing the factors involved, studying them and then using the information to render the best decision at the moment. Similar to reflection but done in a fraction of the time, this is more likely used when choosing from a menu of food or choosing where to sit on the train (the smaller things!).

6. Compliance

The last decision type in our list is compliance, which will lead us to the basis of this chapter. Compliance sees a decision being made that is the most pleasing, comfortable and popular option of those the decision impacts. This is making a decision for a committee to ensure you "keep the peace" or make it a "crowd pleaser." I'll come to why this is so relevant shortly.

As I said, if we had to consciously run these strategies over each of our decisions to pick the best one, we just wouldn't get anything done. Also, of the 35,000 decisions we are making each day, the reality is that less than 1% of them are really going to make a big difference or dent in our journey to success. So, how can we focus our efforts on the 1%? How do we understand which ones fit in those buckets, and, without worrying about applying the strategies above, still make a choice that serves us well? First of all, let's start with the 1% bucket, so we know what we are focusing on.

The 1% Bucket

These are the big or small decisions we make each day that are going to have a profound or compounding impact on our ability to move towards success. Common decisions that fit into this category will be related to finance, time commitments or those that could dent or damage our credibility or authority in our chosen path to success.

Financial decisions might be large decisions that require lump sums of cash (that could otherwise be used more wisely), or potentially smaller commitments over time which could also restrict our ability to move on to the opportunities that serve the right purpose.

Time decisions are similar in the sense that we might be committing large chunks of time to something that distracts us from the path to success, or come with smaller, micro-commitments over a longer period, which results in the same outcome.

When it comes to authority or credibility, these are slightly different and harder to spot, as a negative outcome might only be recognised later, casting doubt on whether we are a good fit or candidate for a new opportunity.

These are all just examples of decisions that would fit into the 1% bucket, but the list is not exclusive to just these. There will be others that can fit in as well. Granted, it can be difficult to tell *which* of the thousand decisions that approach us daily fit into the all-important 1%, especially when you are new to the concept.

Once you understand what these 1% decisions look like, intuition will prevail and present you with the decisions that *could* be "1%ers," so it will be your task to tune in to the decisions presented and identify the ones that truly matter. To help simplify the process, I have developed the tool below, which you can use to quickly assess each potential 1%er and gauge its importance in your success journey.

The 1% Filter

```
                          ┌─────────────────┐
                          │    Decision     │
                          └─────────────────┘
                                   │
                                   ▼
   ┌─────────┐         Is it directly related to         ┌─────────┐
   │   Yes   │◄────────    your success path?   ────────►│   No    │
   └─────────┘                                            └─────────┘
        │                                                      │
        ▼                                                      ▼
 Will the outcome affect      ┌─────────┐        Will the outcome affect
 your success journey?  ─────►│   No    │◄─────  your success journey?
                              └─────────┘
        │                          │                          │
        ▼                          ▼                          ▼
   ┌─────────┐          ┌──────────────────┐            ┌─────────┐
   │   Yes   │          │   Unlikely 1%    │            │   Yes   │
   └─────────┘          └──────────────────┘            └─────────┘
        │                          │                          │
        │                          ▼                          │
        │               ┌──────────────────┐                 │
        └──────────────►│   Likely 1%er    │◄────────────────┘
                        └──────────────────┘
```

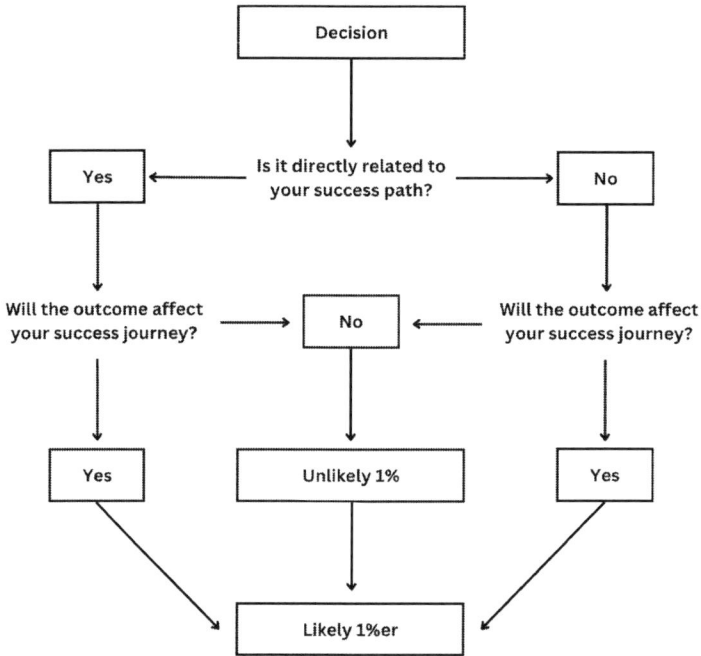

Although it is a simple flow, just by asking yourself these questions, you will be taking those intuitive thoughts and applying logic to them, allowing you to bucket up as many real 1%ers as possible.

There is another layer to this process, which goes above our logical brain and speaks to the primitive self where our desires live, and, if left unchecked, can cloud our decision-making without us even realising. This is where sex and status come into play.

I was introduced to the basis of this concept in the first ever self-help book I ever read, and to this day I still tell people this book changed my life. The book in question is Dale Carnegie's *How to Win Friends and Influence People*, and as it stands today, I have read this book at least ten times over, and every time I am more and more impressed with its contents. The first time I read it I was around 19 years old, which I would categorise now as one of my most unsuccessful years. I lacked direction, motivation, desire and belief that I could be any better than I currently was. That was until (what I now recognise as) a mentor gave me a copy of the book and advised me to read it. This book covers a multitude of useful ways to interact with people, but there is one hidden nugget in the book that spoke to me more than anything else, which was the question, "Why is it, as humans, we do the things we do?"

I have always been able to intuitively get along with people I meet, and I'm often complimented on my ability as a conversationalist. However, my natural reaction is to feel baffled at this, with my internal voice thinking, "Isn't this how everyone acts when they meet people?" Reading the chapter on human behaviour in Carnegie's book filled in a black spot in my understanding of *why* I found it so easy to connect with people: I could identify and very quickly understand what motivates them, and naturally connect with that.

There are many human desires but if we boil them down, the top ones are:

- Health and preservation of life

- Food

- Sleep

- Money and things it will buy

- Life in the hereafter

- Sexual gratification

- The well-being of our children

- A feeling of importance

A lot of the decisions we make on a day-to-day basis will fit into these categories or ones that are similar, because at a base level we are all very similar, although our past gives us more of a bias towards some needs than others. Many of these have been quoted through history to further affirm that these desires exist. For example, John Dewey, one of America's most profound philosophers, once said, "The deepest urge in human nature is 'the desire to be important,'" which highlights just one of the eight in our list. I think this list can be boiled down even further. This is really what stuck with me, and it is confirmed in a quote from Sigmund Freud, (which appears in a form in Carnegie's work) who said, "Everything you and I do springs from two motives: the sex urge and the desire to be great," which is where my chapter title "sex and status" comes from. At the most simplistic level, we can boil all of our desires down to one of these two buckets.

Although a term that might be viewed as crude or lewd, sex is a huge part of our existence, and whether we like it or not, it is a driver in our day-to-day activity. With the rise of social media and a spotlight constantly shone on our everyday lives, the want to be seen and to be desirable is more important now than it has ever been before. Sex in this context doesn't just include the act, but instead the way we attract everyone around us to be interested in our lives. The "sex appeal" we exude carries a huge weight in our day-to-day decision-making.

If sex is the law of desire or attraction, status is the output we push back out into the universe to drive the narrative of who we want to be and how we want to be perceived. Sex and status work in unison, collecting all of the selfless acts, the comments and quips we make, the decisions for the positions we put ourselves in, the messages we put out into the world and the things we do for others. These actions fuel the narrative we are trying to create for ourselves. I've not found a single decision that cannot be put into one of these categories, and I would challenge you to find one. If you dig deep enough into a decision, you'll discover how it serves one of these two human desires and how its use influences the outcomes you achieve. Used in the right way to attract (sex) or emanate success (status), these two desires can align to cause untold results. But used in the wrong way, they can quickly derail you as fast as they can accelerate you. Think of it as the angel and devil sitting on your shoulder. Either way, one of them is going to slam the decision into the bucket; it's your choice who chalks the points up!

Here's an example of using the sex urge to attract people to you: Let's imagine you had a £1,000 bonus that presents itself as spare money, and you are in the stage of your success journey where you are looking to level up to the next position in the company you work for. The angel and devil will be fighting over this money, each trying to influence your decision to spend it in their interest. The angel is presenting a purchase option of an educational course to further your knowledge, and a new suit that will give you a more professional look in the office. On the other hand, the devil is presenting you with the opportunity to put a deposit down on that new sports car or to go on nights out that will look great on your Instagram reel and rub it in the faces of those who are not at your level (#livingmybestlife).

Both fuel the urge, the only difference is the angel is seeing the opportunity to invest and delay gratification, with the devil looking for that instant hit and reward to fuel our desires and be seen in the spotlight. The angel option will likely give us a quicker path to success, ultimately unlocking the devil's desires in the long run, whereas the devil will give you the up-front thrill, but no progression or shortcuts on your journey. So who should you listen to?

Status is no different. Let's consider a scenario where money is not involved: During a meeting with the company's senior leaders, a colleague is midway through a presentation and they make a blunder in the data which could lead to issues later down the line for the company. Our angel is going to pull us to the right decision, which could be to wait for the meeting to complete, and then support our colleague to correct the data, offering a shared win and giving us a status increase with our colleague and the senior leaders for catching the issue.

The devil, on the other hand, would be tempted to highlight the issues during the meeting, which, even if done tactfully, highlights a fault in our colleagues' work, damaging their credibility but allowing us to get the instant gratification and the "pat on the back" status boost we crave.

When we are in a situation where the 1% of decisions rears their head daily, we are going to be presented with the sex and status buckets, and both the angel and the devil will want to have their say. The aim of the game is to stop and understand which one is going to serve us *before* we make the decision so that we can weigh up the pros and cons of each. Sometimes, it's right to let the devil win. I won't discourage you from taking that path when its call is greater than the path to success, as we all need a little instant gratification at times. We just need to make sure that the lion's share of decisions that we make are weighted towards the good choices that build on our journey and serve us in the long run. Treat it like filling up a bank account: When it's full, making the occasional withdrawal is okay.

The more of these choices we win, the more the compound effect will take hold and allow us to accelerate our journey towards success. And just by understanding the sex and status principle, you are already more in control than you ever have been before. As you work through this book, keep this principle in the forefront of your mind. When you find yourself working through the methods of analysing human desires, stop to think: Who is winning the tug of war in your mind – is it the angel or the devil? The more you can work with the angel to win, the faster and easier the climb to success will be.

CHAPTER 3
TO MOVE FORWARDS, LOOK BACK

Imagine if your journey to success was a race. Where would you put the start line? This seems like a stupid question, with the obvious answer being "at the start," right? But where exactly is that?

If you were to run a marathon, would the start be at the beginning of mile one? If you were to race in the Formula One championship, would it be on the starting grid? These seem like obvious places, and in some ways they are correct. They're right because you can't start further forwards than the beginning, because by definition the start is just that. Even if you were to start on mile two of a marathon, it would still be the starting point of your race. So how can the start *not* be at the beginning of your journey?

The reality is that it can't. It's fixed, and whether we want to or not, that first movement forward will begin on the start line, and we are going to be putting a huge amount of energy to get ourselves off the starting line regardless of the direction our success points in.

This chapter isn't going to be able to change these facts, but by its end, your perception of where that start line is will have changed, and you will have a greater understanding of where you are on your journey right now. And the likelihood is, you are a lot further on than you think.

As an entrepreneur, my first real attempt at success was around 2015 when I decided it was time for me to open a real company. I had owned limited companies before this, and made money in them, but this was going to be the first public-facing business that I was going to put my name on for all the world to see and hopefully enjoy.

For this business, I had a partner who, at the time, was a close friend of mine who dreamed of working for himself outside of the corporate world. He had an idea of just how he wanted to do it but wanted my advice and thoughts on it before it kicked off.

We went for a beer in a local bar in Nottingham, which is where I was living at the time. Even to this day, I remember where we sat and what drinks we chose, as to me this was – and still is – a pivotal part of my overall journey to success. My friend shared his idea with me, explaining how he planned to go into business by opening a mobile bar, which he could take to events (his previous career was in the pub industry so it matched his skill set). After looking at the model for a while, the realisation of the start-up costs versus the savings he had available would leave him with a very short runway of funds to stay afloat until the business started making a profit. We stacked the opportunity in a number of ways to try and make it work, but each time we came to the same conclusion: that the risk of failure was a real one unless he took more time to save for the launch.

It was at this point I offered him an alternative idea, which was to go into business together on a model that I had been dreaming of for years, but never had time to execute. It was a street food catering business which had the versatility to work in all walks of the industry, from shops to street events to private functions, and the start-up costs were limited. We agreed that if he could put the time and money into getting it off the ground, I would put my expertise behind the scenes to bring it all together. After raising another glass to the idea, we formed the company and partnership there and then, from Table 3 in the Canal House pub.

Sounds like the start of the journey doesn't it? I thought so too, until about six months into the business when, on a Friday evening after a full week at work, I was making a mess in my home kitchen preparing produce to attend a weekend event. There were cracked eggshells and flour everywhere, and when my wife got home later that evening and found me in what looked like an episode of the Great British Bake Off, she asked me one question that would shape and change my whole perspective.

After a barrage of (no doubt very justified) comments around how, in any normal household, there should not be this level of mess in a kitchen she had deep cleaned the night before, she said, "You must be mad doing all of this after a long week at work, what makes you want to?"

The first thought that popped into my head was money. I wanted to provide a better life for her and at that point, the vision I had for our 2.4 children. As time went on into the evening and 9pm ticked over to 10pm, then to 11pm, with my wife upstairs tucked up in bed and me still scraping a concrete-like mixture of eggs and flour off of our kitchen cupboards, it began to dawn on me that perhaps it was not just money driving me after all.

When I gave it some real thought, money was only about 10% of the reason I did anything. I am just not a financially driven person at all. I had never desired to be a millionaire or been that bothered with materialistic things. Even now, I have only ever made a handful of what I would call "extravagant" purchases, so why the hell did I stay up at 11pm, after a 60-hour work week, preparing for an event that would see me working two more days and likely another 30 hours?

I would love to say I had an epiphany in those moments, that a light bulb went off and I figured it all out, running up the stairs to wake my wife and share the real answer with her. But that didn't happen (and even if it had, it would have been too dangerous to wake her for anything less than the house being on fire!). What it did was spark a change of belief in my mind – one that I wouldn't be able to shift for some time – which was: If I wasn't doing all of this work for money, why was I doing it at all?

The question actually lay unanswered for a few years as I carried on my journey in business and life, taking on more and more as I tried to fill the success bucket without really understanding what I needed or wanted. Even though it was unanswered, the question always hung around as a niggle in my brain, one that I knew needed exploring, but I wasn't sure why or how to go about it. I was finally able to answer the question when I started working with mentors, which forced me to really dig deeper into my overall "why." Why do I do the things I do? What is it that drives me? Back in 2015, I knew it wasn't money that was driving me, even though it was a great perk of being a business owner. I was getting something else from it, something that gave me more joy and more purpose.

Today, it's clear to me that the reason I pushed myself consistently towards success was actually for two things. The first was to help others in any way that I could, either directly or indirectly; and the second was for validation from those close to me and the world around me, to tell me I was good enough. These are two pretty deep thoughts that took me years to hone in on, but not because there were buried and suppressed parts of me that needed to be discovered, and more because I didn't know I needed to search for them in the first place.

Since understanding these two purposes and drivers exist, I have been able to multiply tenfold the results of my efforts, because now I know what drives me to do the things I do. I have been able to apply that traction to a clearer and more defined path that serves both me and those closest to me, while avoiding distraction from all the other things that might serve those needs without seeing results.

So, where do you think I found the answers to my questions of "why"? Were they in my messy kitchen as I prepared for events in my first company? Were they in the bar in Nottingham in 2015? To find that answer, we actually need to look decades before, all the way back to the environment I grew up in.

As I mentioned previously, I was the youngest in our household by 18 months, and also the most easygoing. I was the second and last born into our family unit and in our early years, my brother was more demanding of attention than I was. He was the child that didn't sleep at night, robbing hours of rest from our weary parents, the typical difficult baby and toddler that comes to mind that we've all encountered at some stage. This meant there wasn't room for me to be the same, so instead I became the polar opposite, blending into the background because there simply wasn't any more attention to grab.

For my parents, this was ideal, as they were already stretched thin. Me fitting in was essential in avoiding additional stress that could have led to nervous breakdowns if I had been just like my brother. Obviously, I remember none of this, and I can only go off what I have been told, like the story I have already shared with you of being called "baby" for the first year of my life. Remember, that's not because my parents didn't name me, it's just because they spent all of their time speaking to my brother and referring to me as "the baby." "Mind the baby," or "Baby is trying to sleep, please be quiet" would be the phrases thrown around often. This was the start of many years spent being in the shadows, just outside of the spotlight, which suited me fine. I enjoyed being the happy child that made people smile and laugh.

As a child, when asked what I wanted to do when I grew up, it was always the same answer: "I want to make people smile and laugh." It quickly became my core purpose – and that's because I was good at it! My brother had the ability to capture the attention of any room, putting on shows and acts to entertain people, whereas I had the ability to connect with people's hearts, which quickly became the fuel and fire in mine. This dynamic continued into my teen years, with my brother taking centre stage like a performer to entertain the masses, while I worked the audience by connecting with them and making them smile and feel special. We are a bit of a dream team when we work together on this!

It's these experiences, alongside other influences and lessons I learned as a child, that made me who I am today, giving me a natural ability from a young age to connect with people of all ages and backgrounds effortlessly. This ability allows me to observe a room or a person and, with a high success rate, understand what motivates them and how I can add value and happiness to their lives.

I wouldn't for a second change who I am because of my upbringing. I am grateful to all of the parental figures in my life for how I was raised. The opportunities that have been presented to me in my life so far are a direct reflection of their efforts in crafting me as a person. They made me into a well-rounded and caring human being, which now, being a parent myself, I realise is no easy feat, and one that takes huge sacrifice from all involved.

However, there is a famous saying that goes, "For every gift, there is a curse," and I believe this is more applicable to upbringing than to any other context. I was gifted with the abilities above by the environment I was raised in, but living in the shadow of someone who demands attention means that, unless you generate your own, you spend a considerable amount of time not receiving the same level of attention. When this becomes a constant in your life, and your attention comes from the effort you put into being noticed, you naturally believe that to be accepted, you have to serve the people around you to be worthy of their time and admiration.

I would and still do spend hours ensuring those around me are safe, secure, happy and looked after. I would go to the ends of the earth – even to my own detriment – if it meant I could be the person who enabled someone else's joy and happiness. There are two ways this has manifested in me. The first is when I withdraw into the shadows and lose the belief that I am good enough. This happened in my final year of education; I lost the belief that I was good enough so I simply stopped pushing. I failed my exams, left school and got a job in a local pub as a pot wash. I gained weight, stopped taking care of my appearance and essentially started a downward spiral. Even during this time, while I was rapidly declining personally, I still pushed to be good enough and be accepted by those around me, and every career path I chose during this time, I started at the bottom and rose the ranks to as high as I could before moving on. From pot wash to head chef, from warehouse operative to account manager, from salesman to area manager. The desire to impress and serve carried me forward, but the promotions and "success" never fulfilled me, so the downward personal spiral would continue.

The second way this manifests is by taking on too much, supporting and helping too many people and eventually burning out. This is a common trait in entrepreneurs in general, who wear burnout and being busy like a badge of honour, considering it a rite of passage to success. I used to think it was impressive to have three jobs or run six companies at the same time, and for years this gave me a false sense of validation that, again, I was "enough" to those around me. During this time I would still go out of my way for others, dropping everything to help anyone who needed it, whether they were close to me or barely known. I would help just to get that validation of being accepted.

The reason and main driver for both of these ways of living was all based on my personal battle with believing I was not enough in life. Was I worthy of the spotlight? Were those I loved proud of me?

For me success wasn't about the money or sex appeal; it was about the status of being accepted. For years I didn't understand this, yet it took one simple question from my wife to nudge that door open just wide enough that it would never close again. One question that would lead to a path of discovery instrumental not just in my success, but in my enjoyment of both the journey and the destination.

So, this is your opportunity to open up that door, to truly understand where this journey of success began for you, so you can uncover your "why." Everyone's starting points and "why" will be different, which is why I cannot tell you exactly where to look. But what I *can* do is start you on the path to discovery, and once you commit to pulling that thread, the more you pull, the more you will learn. It all starts with these three questions:

1) What motivates you more:

   a) Money

   b) Knowing you can (for yourself)

   c) Showing others you can (to prove you are enough)

   d) Desire to help (others)

   e) Desire for power

2) When was the first time you remember feeling elated from a success?

   a) Earliest memory

   b) Early childhood

   c) School

   d) In a first relationship

   e) Later in life

3) When you felt that way, who was the first person you wanted to tell?

    a) A parent

    b) A family member

    c) A partner

    d) Someone you looked up to (in work, home, life, etc.)

    e) Anyone who would listen

    f) Other

Once you have your three answers, they will lead you to a feeling, a specific point in time and a person or group of people who were important for you to tell. This is a starting point for exploring why you were driven and who influenced your desire to succeed in that way. From here you will be able to dig further and deeper into the route of the reason as to your "why."

This can take time, and you'll want to always look further than you think is needed, as usually this is where epiphanies live. You will know when you find one because it feels like it suddenly all makes sense, like you have been staring at one of those paintings that you have to look at with your eyes squinted and your head at an angle until a picture appears from the squiggles and lines. (I've never been able to get those to work!) Just trust the process, and when you discover a pattern in your thoughts and behaviours, pull harder on the thread to discover more.

For me, looking back helped shape my understanding of how I became the way I am, and why I now act how I do. It also helped me attract people who were the complete opposite of me, which in turn helped me realise that I thought completely differently to everyone around me.

My wife and I are very different people, she is the ying to my yang. I live to serve others while she would much rather be served. She comes from a single-child household where all of the attention was on her as she grew up and she wanted for nothing. When our lives became more entwined as our relationship progressed, she just couldn't understand why I put so much effort into being accepted by others. She continually questioned my reasoning (which nudged the door open more and more), and as an outsider looking in, it was a lot clearer for her what was driving me to impress others and be of service.

It took me many years before I finally decided to confront what was on the other side of the door and to understand my real "why," which allowed me to change my behaviour. It took me so long to realise that the curse I had was not and never would really serve me.

The reality is, when we decide to set out on the journey to success, we are not pulling up to the start line and getting ready for the klaxon to sound. Instead, we are jumping on a train that has been powering forward for as long as we have been in existence. We are simply putting ourselves in the driver's seat to control where it takes us to next. To move forward effectively, we must look back. By studying the tracks the train has already travelled on, we will better understand what fuels the engine and turns the wheels, and realise whether the track we are on is or isn't serving us. Once we are able to apply that traction to the track *we* choose, we can gain more momentum and speed than we ever thought possible, and it will all be in the right direction.

For me, I needed to confront the fact that everything I was doing in my life was either driven by a desire for validation and love, a want to prove that I wasn't in the shadows or second best, or by a belief that I wasn't good enough and that I wasn't loved or accepted. Now, on the other side of the discovery, I can see the curse I was feeling was only relevant and real to me, and that to everyone else they had no perception that it even existed. I was fighting a curse that I had manifested because of how I felt in the early years of my life, without even realising it.

In the next chapter, we look at how we can challenge the perceptions we have had for years and how we can have those difficult conversations to unlock the realities that exist outside of the confines of our own beliefs. Just know that even if you don't feel like you have set out and taken the first steps to your success, the likelihood is you have already completed half the journey. Now all that's left is to make sure you are heading in the right direction.

CHAPTER 4
IS THAT WHAT
YOU MEANT?

From the moment we're born, communication is key to our survival. Even before a language is learned to articulate wants and needs, a baby can communicate with a simple (and often loud!) cry for help. Whether they're hungry, in pain, in need of attention or in danger, a baby can adapt its cry to draw attention to a parent who is hopefully nearby to aid and support.

This is human communication in its most raw and simplistic form, and it happens from Day One. Yet, the more time that elapses, the more complicated communication becomes for us, and the more likely it is that not using this skill correctly could land us in trouble!

How often do you find yourself staring into thin air, enjoying a daydream filled with all the finer things in life, when someone calls your name and asks if you are listening to what they are saying? That rush of panic, the cold sweat, while you desperately try to remember the last thing you heard them say before you drifted away to somewhere nicer. Then, you try your hardest to save face by responding with something you heard earlier in the conversation, in the hope that the topic hadn't changed too much while you were off.

As humans, we were given five incredibly useful senses, allowing us to touch, see, taste, smell and hear (even if sometimes we are caught short on the last one!). We allow these senses to guide us in our everyday lives, relying on them to keep us safe but also to enjoy. They enhance our existence, allowing us to learn new and interesting ways to interact with our world.

They were also created to keep us safe, and millions of years ago, when we had to keep an eye out for predators or hunt for food to eat, they served our species incredibly well. Without them, we would not have been able to survive what the world threw at us, stunting our chances to evolve. This no doubt would have made it impossible to have all of the fantastic things we have today.

Our senses now best serve us as a means of enjoyment rather than protection, allowing us to taste fine and exquisite foods, hear and enjoy new and innovative types of music, and see and appreciate the truly beautiful parts of our world, which might have been overshadowed by caution and trepidation before. Now that our senses are no longer overloaded with the need to protect us from imminent threats, the shift brings many benefits and joys, but also introduces an unexpected issue. This problem often goes unnoticed but can significantly influence our entire existence and belief system. How can our ability to hear sometimes lead us down paths that have never and should never exist? To understand, we need to look a little deeper than the senses and consider what they're connected to, which is one of the best data-crunching computers found amongst living creators: the brain.

The brain was designed to work in sync with all of our senses, constantly analysing our environment as each sense fired off hundreds of bits of information as we moved about the world, all while it seamlessly adjusted our behaviours to take advantage of situations we found ourselves in. Our brain's ability to do this is one of the reasons we have been able to adapt over time into the civilizations we are today, sitting at the top of the food chain having seen off most natural threats. For the most part, we're secure in our ability to not only survive, but to *thrive* in our existence, with no want or need to worry about predators, and with sound knowledge of where we can get our next meal. This means our brain's ability to keep us safe is no longer needed to the degree it was designed, and its capacity can be focused elsewhere.

We now fuel our brains with other information, giving us the power to manifest outcomes, thoughts, dreams, creations and more in great detail, which is partly where our problem starts. The brain can create ideas and concepts that shape and guide us for months, years, decades and sometimes even our lifetimes, all from what our senses pick up from the world around us.

Without careful consideration of the inputs we are providing our brains, we leave ourselves quite vulnerable to living in a reality that only exists inside of our heads, based on how we listen and interpret the world around us. This leads us down a path that is only in existence in our own mind. I experienced this myself when I believed I had to prove myself to the world and those around me – all because I allowed my perception of being in the shadows to shape how I heard what people around me said.

Let me explain how our ability to hear can often lead us down these roads, and the consequences we could face by allowing it to happen. We are going to be focusing on the sense of hearing, and for the context of this book, we are going to assume that hearing also includes what we read with our internal voice (text messages, notes, emails, etc.). First, let's look at the definition of the verb hearing:

> **Hear, v.** To receive or become conscious of a sound using your ears.

This is the rudimentary form of how we interact with sound, and what our brain allows us to do with these sounds is to listen. To hear is not a learned ability, and for the majority of us, hearing is something we are able to do from birth. *Listening*, however, is something we learn over time. From an early age, we learn to listen to our parents as they warn us away from danger. We listen to teachers and other sources of education as we learn how to process tone and context. Over time, we build our own ability to listen (with some having mastered the skill better than others).

So, if we have the ability to hear from birth and learn how to listen and communicate with others as we grow and develop, how can we end up getting it so wrong? The problem this relates to is when we hear (and listen) to words from those around us, and without questioning how the words are intended, we build our own picture of what they mean. For most people, this happens all too often. They will be told something (usually by someone they care deeply about), and it will have a profound effect on their lives, even if the comment or conversation was not intended to be interpreted in that way.

These words, conversations or comments can occur in a moment, lasting less than a few seconds as they are spoken. But to the person who hears them, the impact they have on their entire existence can be profound. The words might be said flippantly, with very little thought about their impact. When questioned, the person who spoke them might not even remember saying them, as the words held little value to them. Yet, to those who heard them, it might be an event they relive and replay in their minds over and over, remembering exactly how it made them feel and the path it led them down.

Don't get me wrong, there will also be times when someone will have said something purposefully to impact your life (for good and bad reasons), and the aim of this chapter is to challenge the ones that we heard incorrectly, that have gone on to shape our (incorrect) perceptions and realities.

You will have already had these moments in your own life, and by the end of this chapter I hope you will be able to:

- Realise what was said to you and how you have allowed it to shape your path.

- Challenge the perception you had of the conversation or words spoken.

- Reset the perceptions you once made and replace them with new ones.

- Learn from these moments and improve your ability to question these moments.

I have had many of these moments throughout my life, from childhood right through to the last few years. In each of these instances, I have had to revisit and challenge the conversations I once had (and misunderstood) to truly understand them. The ones that I found have shaped my way of being the most are almost exclusively from my childhood, and are usually from conversations with my immediate family.

This isn't a coincidence, as I was lucky enough to grow up in a loving home where I genuinely cared about what they all thought of me. I value their opinions and take to heart what they say more than if others were to say the same things. In essence, to me it mattered a lot more what my family thought of me as I grew up than what others did.

To show you how these moments might exist in your life, I will share one from my early teenage years that set me on a course that, if left unchecked, would have resulted in you not reading this book today. Put simply, that path would have prevented me from achieving what I have, and I would never have dreamt of writing this book.

For this, we are going to travel back in time to 26th August 2004, to a 16-year-old version of me who was working full-time in a café about 10 miles from my house. I felt a mix of nervous excitement and trepidation, and I remember being in the back room of the café, which was small and stuffy, with stainless steel kitchen worktops. I was prepping the egg mayonnaise sandwich filler (which wasn't helping the nervous, sick feeling), and it was one of those days when you do everything you can think of to keep yourself busy. Yet, when you look at the clock after what feels like an hour, you realise that only ten minutes have passed.

The reality was, there were another five million 16-year-olds in the UK that day probably feeling exactly the same way that I was. Why? Because it was the day they released the GCSE results in 2004. This was meant to be one of the most important days of my life, one that I had been building up to for some time, as had all of my friends. The hopes and dreams of a generation were in the balance – and I was one of them!

The difference in me already was that I had adopted a strong work ethic early on, and had accepted to work that day rather than collecting the results myself. So, we had planned for my mum to collect them on my behalf, drive to work to meet me and then open the results together. I didn't give much thought to it at the time, that it might have been a nice experience for me to open my results amongst friends, but my focus was more around earning money and getting a head start in life (likely to prove to others that I could).

The day ticked on, and I remember listening to the news on the radio, hearing about all of the results that had been opened and the UK averages that were being achieved. I was excited but nervous about what was to come, as I had never been great with exams. I was and still am a kinaesthetic learner, and got the best results through "learning on the job" rather than the theoretical or book learnings that others preferred. I have also never been fantastic at sitting exams. The pressure was something I didn't take well to, even though day-to-day I was a bright young lad. So I should have been expecting average results. C's would be fantastic and anything above would have been phenomenal and a true reflection of how hard I had worked on my revision and studying.

I would be the second in our family to get GCSE results, with my brother completing his the year before, getting exemplary A and A* results across the board. So the bar had already been set incredibly high. In my mind, if I could get even close to an A it would be celebrated, so either way, the pressure was high. My nerves were getting even shorter, and if I had to cut up another boiled egg in the hot backroom, I thought I might just pass out. So when my mum finally appeared at the cafe window and beckoned me outside, it was a relief to know the wait was almost over.

The cafe was on the corner of a busy pedestrian street which led into an arcade. The room I had been prepping in had a rear door that connected to the arcade via a back door, so I rushed out to meet her and we both took a seat on the adjacent shop's window ledge. She handed me the envelope and instantly I felt sick, knowing that once I opened it we would all know the result and there would be no going back.

I peeled back the envelope flap which had been sealed shut and pried out the piece of paper that was within. I finally had my results in my hand and my eyes began to scan down the letters marked against each subject I had taken.

Mathematics	C
English literature	E
English Language	D
Double Science	2 x B
Spanish	F
IT	U
Geography	G

Now before I tell you what happened next, there is a reason I have gone into so much detail when telling you this story. I wanted you to fully understand how the 16-year-old version of me was feeling in the build-up to the opening of my results, how much I could feel the weight of expectation on my shoulders and where I had already set the bar for myself before getting to this point.

So, how do you think my feelings matched my expectations of the results? My aim was to get close to an A, not achieve one. If we look at the results above, I had accomplished that not once, but twice, with two B's in Science shining out of the page. All of the core subjects are in reasonable shape too, with C's and D's, which, for someone of my ability and belief system at the time, was a reasonable achievement. However, there is one fact that we cannot ignore: the E, F, U, and G also lined up for judgement alongside what I saw as some diamonds shining through the rough.

So at this point, I had no idea of the reaction I was going to get for these results, but I was hopeful. I proudly handed them to my Mum so she could also analyse them before passing her verdict, and as you can likely imagine, it was one of those moments where the world seemed to stop. A second felt like an hour in time as the world seemed to go into slow motion. She scanned the results for probably the fifth time in her mind before the first two words left her mouth: "Oh, darling."

Without me telling you the tone, this could be read as a joyful remark of pride for the highs I had reached in my pursuit of the B grades or as her teeing up a remark that would console me. So, here are the next words she said to me when she finally looked up at me from the paper in her hand:

"Don't worry, you can always be a dustman."

As these words washed over me, they instantly forged a new core memory deep within my being. This moment in my mind was forever labelled as sad and filled with disappointment, and as I sat in that alleyway, smelling like warm eggs and mayonnaise, I began to cry.

That moment, those words and that feeling was the start of me altering my own self-beliefs, transforming my mindset into someone who would achieve nothing in life. For years this sent me on a path of doing exactly that. I woke up that morning feeling like I could take my place as a success in the eyes of the world, and went to bed feeling like I had let my family down and I was always going to be the boy who tried but could never succeed.

Why? Because I had heard seven words, and without questioning them, I allowed them to cement and manifest in my mind as a new belief. To give you context of just how long I allowed this belief to haunt me, I didn't question these words or their meaning until I was around 26 years old, a full 10 years after they were spoken. In reality, I probably would have never questioned those words fully had it not been for my wife pushing open that internal door, and my first ever mentor working with me on my self-limiting beliefs (which to this day, I am eternally grateful for).

Let's have a look at the words from another perspective: my mum's. I should say my mum has nothing against the dustbin men and was and is a superbly loving mother whom I adore immensely. So why did she choose these words at such a critical point in my life, and did she know they were going to affect me so deeply? Of course, she didn't. In fact, years later, when we did speak about the moment, she couldn't even remember saying them. This was because, to her, the words were, quite frankly, irrelevant.

She remembered the terrible 30-minute drive from the school to my place of work, dreading that the results weren't as good as I hoped they would be, not versus her expectations. Sitting in that alleyway as she scanned the results, she wasn't digesting them before passing judgement, she was wondering how I might be feeling and how she could make the situation lighter and support me as a mother and a friend. Without a great deal of personal work, we are pre-programmed to focus on the negatives and the potential risks and pitfalls, as it's what kept us alive in the early years of humanity.

And it still exists within us now. My mum could see the F, U, G, and E and wanted to make me feel better, so the words, "Don't worry, you can always be a dustman," were a light-hearted remark to make the situation easier for both of us.

I allowed a light-hearted remark intended to lighten my mood to guide a decade of my life's decisions – all because I didn't question them. If I had simply asked my mum in the moment, or in the days and weeks that followed the conversation, "Do you really think that's all I will be able to achieve?" she would have quickly reset my beliefs and changed that 10-year trajectory. Instead, I allowed it to bore down into my soul, and it became a part of me until I was shown I didn't have to hold onto them anymore.

You will have these core limiting beliefs deep within your soul too, and to move forwards in your pursuit of success, it is time to crack open the internal filing cabinet you have shoved them all into and let them go. And here's how we are going to do it:

In the previous chapter, we began exploring the past to better understand our journey so far, and although the things we discover will have led us to where we are, it is important to only hold onto the ones that are still able to serve us. The ones that will no longer serve us are the ones that are now hurting our progress and holding us back, or that are hindering the relationships we have built with the people they are attached to.

Firstly, we need to identify what these limiting beliefs are, because unlike in the previous chapter, where we looked at the choices we have made so far, we now need to look at what led us to make those choices in the first place. What are the limiting beliefs, the core beliefs or the opinions about ourselves that we hold and where did they come from? There are two ways I use to weed these beliefs out, and the more in touch you are with yourself, the easier they are to uncover as you use this first method, which is simply to create a list of all the things we believe to be true about ourselves, such as:

- I've never been good with (reading, writing, computers, people, etc.)
- I'm always terrible at (exams, travelling, overeating, etc.)
- I'll never get (promoted, recognised, married, etc.)

The list could be endless variations of these, but they are all limiting beliefs that are holding us back for the simple reason that we believe them. What we believe, at our core, will always be true to us and will manifest in what we do. There's a reason people say manifesting with positive affirmations works, because if you genuinely believe what you are saying, it can come true. Well, the same applies to the negatives. Our bodies and minds will push us to live the negative beliefs, and they become our reality.

Now, if you have sat down with a pen and paper and tried to write these for yourself and only come up with a small list, it's time for the second method. This method involves asking others for their perceptions, which removes the ability to filter the list yourself. People close to us can often see things we might not, and if we ask the right people, they will provide a list that is both considered and most likely true.

So, I challenge you to get your phone out, head over to your favourite messaging app and send the following message to people whose opinion you value and who have your best interests at heart:

"What are the three things that I honestly believe about myself that, whether they are true or not, are holding me back in life?"

Wait for the replies to come in and add these to your list, too. You will find that, if you ask the right people, not only will they know you better than you think, but they might also be able to show you some of your blind spots. Now, you will have a list of beliefs that you can begin to link back to the moments that created them. The deeper you explore, the closer to the root you will reach, and it is only there that we can explore the moments that caused them in the first place. The more recent the root of the belief, the more likely it is still surface level and it will take some considerable self-work to get to the roots of the beliefs that can sometimes span most of your lifetime.

It's important to understand that the misheard or held moments that are only surface level now, might not directly affect our day-to-day decisions and can mostly be shrugged off. However, the problem is if they are not dealt with and challenged, they can bore down deeper to become a core belief that will change our path and overall belief system.

Whether it's a deep core belief or something that is currently surface-level, we are going to use the same technique to better understand the truth behind our perception, which is to ask a simple question after setting the scene as you remember it. Utilise the "Mention and Meaning" framework below.

FRAMEWORK OVERVIEW

- Remind them of the moment in time

- Remind them of the words you heard

- Tell them how you felt & how you understood their words

ASK THE QUESTION

"Is that what you meant?"

To use this framework, follow the step-by-step guide below:

Step 1: The Moment

Begin the conversation by setting the scene. Describe it as completely as you can, touching on aspects like where you were, why you were there, how important the moment was to you and who else was present. The idea is to allow this information to jog their memory to take them back to the same point in time. Once you have done this, confirm they remember the moment.

Step 2: What You Heard

This is where you are going to remind them of what you believe you heard them say. This is the pivotal moment, so commit to telling them exactly what you believe you heard them say and how you took the words.

Step 3: How You Understood

In this step, you are going to tell them how you understood the words you heard and, in the context you heard them, how they made you feel.

Step 4: Ask What They Meant

You are now going to ask them the question, "Is that what you meant?" and allow the conversation that follows to either confirm your understanding or reshape your understanding of it. Be prepared for the person to not remember what they meant at the time, especially if this happened some time ago. If this is the case, ask them what they would mean by those words if they were to say them now, or how would they respond now if the conversation were to happen again.

This framework will enable you to start the conversation that can help you grow, as you question fundamental truths you are holding about yourself, based on moments and conversations from your past.

Here's how it would look when applied to the moment in my past I shared earlier:

Step 1: "Mum, do you remember when you collected my GCSE results for me and met me at work?"

[Pause]

Step 2: "And once we had both read the results, you said not to worry and that I could always be a dustman?"

[Pause]

Step 3: "Because when you said that, I remember feeling crushed and it made me believe I honestly wouldn't be able to be anything more than just that. Is that what you meant?"

It's a very simple framework, but when applied to an emotional conversation, it can be quite hard to use. The reason? Fear of what the other person will say. There is a reality where they might confirm your beliefs – which could hurt, especially if you have respect and love for the person you are asking.

Now, everyone is allowed to have an opinion, which will be made up of constructs and moments from their own past, and sometimes these will differ from our own, which is perfectly fine. The great news though, is that there is only one person in control of what you believe, and that is *you*. You do not have to believe or buy into the person's opinion, no matter how much they mean to you, or how much the opinion means to them.

It is also not just one reality that can come from the conversation – other outcomes can be a lot more positive. Sometimes, the person might not even remember the words you are recalling, as they didn't think or mean for it to be a pivotal moment. They might also remember the words but have meant them in another way entirely, or you might have misheard them in the first place.

When it is one of these realities that comes to light, the conversations that happen afterwards can be quite powerful, and you can ask the person questions that cannot only remove an incorrect belief, but also help start to build on a new version of yourself through clarity on what was meant, and what that person actually thinks you are capable of.

In my case, my mum always believed I could do anything I wanted, I just needed to apply myself to that dream and it could become a reality. Had I confronted what I heard all those years ago, my path and journey could have been very different. You might have even been able to read this book 10 years sooner.

Truthfully though, I wouldn't change the path I took even if I could. It made me who I am today, it led me to meet the fantastic people I have met throughout my life and it led me to marry the most amazing woman, have the most beautiful children and be in a position where I have created a life by design. We should never wish to change the past, only to better understand the moments it holds so we can navigate the future more efficiently to great health, wealth and happiness.

So, my task to you for this chapter is to start to challenge some of the things you have been holding onto that fit your existing beliefs. If you start with surface-level moments and get comfortable challenging where they originated from, you will quickly realise that it is not a conversation to be feared. Instead, these conversations present an opportunity to heal self-created wounds and repair and strengthen relationships that could drift apart due to simple misunderstandings.

By addressing them now and fixing past perceptions, you will get better at avoiding future misunderstandings altogether by simply asking at the moment, "What do you mean by that?" This simple question will play a bigger role in your overall success than you can possibly imagine.

Hopefully, after this deep dive into uncovering misheard comments and conversations that shaped misconceptions and false limiting beliefs, you will have gained more insight into yourself and what drives these beliefs. The process will take time, and you should treat the Mention and Meaning Framework like an internal mental muscle—the more you work on it, the stronger your ability to maximise your results using it.

The results of using it frequently will pay dividends in the long run and help support you on your journey to success.

CHAPTER 5
WHAT IS REAL SUCCESS

So now that we know where we sit with health, wealth and happiness, our pasts and preconceptions that led us to where we are, and how to accelerate our success by asking difficult questions, it's time to focus on what *real* success actually looks like. It might surprise you that before we even get to success, there are other things that need to be considered.

If we are going to truly understand where our journey is going, the understanding of success and its contributing factors is essential. We will start, again, with the definition:

> **Success, n.** The accomplishment of an aim or purpose.

My perception is that for most people reading this book, this definition will not be a shock or surprise, as success is a common word that is seen in so many places. Whether it be in work, fitness, parenting, schooling, cooking – the list is endless and success is usually measured when we reach an end result. So when we set out on any task, we usually have a goal in mind that will dictate whether it is a success or failure.

Let's take cooking as an example. Imagine you have a group of friends coming round for an evening of catching up, food and fun. As you prepare for the approaching evening, you already have the success metric of the food being enjoyed in your mind's eye, and this is where your journey begins.

First, you must pick the menu, taking into account the variables that stand before you for the ultimate enjoyment of the group. The group might include someone who doesn't eat meat, another who has an allergy or religious beliefs that prohibit some ingredients. Here is where the complexities of success start to take hold as you select what you believe to be the perfect menu.

You "float" the idea within the group and look for confirmation that your choice is a good one, and once you have the thumbs up, you progress to the next stage: shopping for the ingredients. You will need to turn what started as an idea, into the reality of a dinner party being in full flow with the food being enjoyed by all. You select the best ingredients for the dish with a balance of affordability, flavour and quality in mind, and then head home to start to bring the dream to life for your friends and family to enjoy.

The oven's heated, the pans are prepped and the first ingredients hit the heat. Their aromas fill the air as your guests begin to arrive – it is the first hint of the meal they will notice. You work tirelessly, calling on the collective experiences you've had in the kitchen to make the most of the tools and tastes you have in front of you to bring to life the image of the dish you have in your mind. The cooking is complete, and your guests are taking their seats at a well-laid table, the wine is being poured as you bring together all of your efforts in the kitchen by presenting the food in a way that's the most palatable and pretty to your guests.

If you are like me, you stand back from what now used to be your kitchen counter, but now resembles a freshly burgled house, with draws half open, every utensil and pan strewn all over the worktop and an apron covered in splatters and sauces to the point that it could be mistaken for evidence in a murder case. You pause for breath as you look down at what you spent the last few hours creating and one or two feelings wash over you.

The first is SUCCESS! You have *nailed* the brief. The food smells, tastes and looks great and you are over the moon with the result. You take a few snaps for social media before proudly moving from the kitchen to the dining table, with a beaming grin of pride as you put the meals in front of your nearest and dearest.

Or the second: FAILURE! How has this happened?! The food doesn't look remotely like the Pinterest photo and the smell and taste aren't stacking up either! We've all seen it before, where someone attempts to make a birthday cake with an online recipe, and rather than it looking like a hedgehog it looks like roadkill. Now, your dish is joining its ranks – you are going to be a laughing stock! You begrudgingly walk into the room where your friends are gathered, looking hungry and hopeful, and before the plates even hit the tablecloth cloth you are making excuses. "This hasn't turned out well" or "It shouldn't look like this." You feel dejected, embarrassed and like you've let your guests down, wishing you chose something simpler to cook or just ordered takeaway instead.

Have you been in either of these situations before? If you are not a cook, replace the example with a similar process and I'm sure the feelings and sentiments will feel the same. You will either feel like you are on cloud nine, or that the world needs to swallow you up, and for the most part you will have experienced both. The interesting thing though, is that this isn't the end of the journey.

Before we get to that, I want you to consider how this is a micro instance of success. When you zoom out a little and look at the moment over a week, month or year, the further you retract your focus, the less significant the success or failure is. When we experience these moments and the categories we place them in, we often feel at that exact moment in time that nothing else matters except success or failure. But in reality, whether we succeed or fail in creating what we set out to, they are just brush strokes on a much larger canvas. Journeys to success span over a multitude of time frames, from days to weeks, weeks to months, months to years and sometimes even decades. The longer the journey to success, the more gravity and bearing the result will have on how we feel and how long that feeling lasts.

So let's get back to our example, where you are going to explore the rest of your journey to success or failure, and to begin we will look at your perceived failure. You've put the dish together and it just did not meet your expectations. You are disappointed, dejected and feeling embarrassed in front of your guests. You've put down the plates while apologising for the failure, and one or two friends have probably already consoled you with comments like, "It's fine, it looks great," or "Oh, don't worry, you've put so much effort in it I'm sure it will be lovely." If you have friends like mine, the banter has already started too. You likely will not believe the comments your friends have made because, in your head, you have already decided they are not going to enjoy the meal. After all, it's not as you wanted it to be.

Your friends pick up their forks and politely put the food in their mouths to start the meal, and the silence descends... To your surprise, they pick up another forkload and dig in. The noises of happy guests start to fill the air and the comments of, "This is delicious," and "MATE, this is bagging!" start to flow, and you pick up your own fork and take a bite. It might not be the success you envisioned, but you begin to enjoy the meal too. When your friends reassure you, again your comments of, "But it needed more salt," and "It should have been cooked slightly less," are dismissed and you begin to feel slightly less of a failure and slightly more like a success. As your friends enjoy the meal more and the evening goes on, the feelings of failure are as if they never existed, and instead are replaced by an evening that everyone has enjoyed, with little to no importance being placed on how you felt when you first left the kitchen.

So now, let's look at the other end of the spectrum, your success! You nailed the brief, you've plated up your masterpiece, taken your four or five photos from different angles for social media and proudly carried your dishes to the table. As you lay the meals in front of your guests and join them at the table, you beckon them to tuck in and the meal begins, with you feeling proud and content. As each guest begins to eat, you notice one friend picks up the salt and starts to add it to their meal, while another asks if there is any sauce like mustard or mayo. You notice that no one mentioned how nice the meal is even though they are all eating it. You probe, asking each guest what they think of the meal, and the first comes back with "It's nice, just needed a little seasoning," then the second, "I've never had it made this way before, it's usually spicier." The other answers are all similar to, "Yeah it's good, thank you."

Suddenly, you've fallen off cloud nine, going from feeling like your dish was a triumph to feeling shaken by your guest's comments and second-guessing the success. The feeling of elation and pride has been removed and replaced with feelings of uncertainty, confusion and ultimately: failure.

How could both of these emotions and results be turned around so quickly, with the highs and the lows twisting around like an emotional rollercoaster? What do you think it was that affected our results so highly? Why did we not see it coming? This is the second layer of success and one that affects us more than our own perceptions of the result, which is the perceptions of those around us. The closer they are to us, the more their opinion of our success will matter, to the point where, if not managed correctly, it will trump our own views tenfold. So, if they mean so much to us, why would they bring the fault up at all? This is where ego comes into play.

Ego, n. A person's sense of self-esteem or self-importance.

Our ego is a misunderstood part of our mental make-up, with the term being bandied around in many different ways. You might have heard it being used to describe an "egotistical person," which is a person who is self-obsessed or self-absorbed. But the reality is we all have an ego, and like the framework from our last chapter, it can be trained like a muscle in the body to have "strength."

Ego strength and its varieties can be studied in depth in other books, where it has been described as having up to eight varieties or being linked to our childlike states. For the purpose of looking at success, we are going to view our and others' egos as one complete form.

Ego strength, n. An individual's capacity to maintain his/her own identity despite physiological pain, distress, turmoil and conflict between internal forces, as well as the demands of reality.

So why do our own and others' egos play such a large part in our success, and how can we work to make sure we have the ego strength needed to manage the feelings created internally when we and others find fault in our results? We first need to understand why we have an ego in the first place, what it can do to serve us and what it can do to hurt us.

The mind is often seen as a complete vessel with infinite space to be filled with knowledge, love, memories and understanding. If you consider the billions of minds in existence and the expanse they all cover collectively, it would be logical to assume that there would be overlap between them at some points, with shared space felt by a multitude of others. The reason this is not the case is our ego is designed to pin us to one point of reference (our own point), and we look outward towards these overlaps from our own point of view. Although we spend time building bridges and connections through talking, thinking and sharing thoughts and ideas with others, our ego sets boundaries from true togetherness on a mass scale by keeping us separated on our own distinct mental island. We only usually see this broken when we meet a life partner and our love for them outweighs our own ego (even though it still usually crops up and lands us in an argument with that partner every once in a while).

The ego survives on shaky ground, and to continue its existence and hold over our mental space, it must bring our own thoughts into question. It does this subtly and appears as the voice in our head asking questions that start with, "But what if...?" or "Are you certain...?" The less trained our ego strength is, the more we listen to it, even when the evidence is pointing us in the right direction. Our egos are also the part of our mind that not only picks fault with ourselves, but with others, too. We might think that when we receive criticism from others, it is meant to dent our ego. We might also feel that when we provide our loved ones "constructive feedback," we are supporting them to improve, but unchecked, it might be our ego serving its own self-wants and needs.

This is because when we find fault with others, there is a silent inference that we are, in fact, better than that person. Although that might give us some level of gratification on a subconscious level, the existence of that gratification is solely reliant on the fault being present in someone else, which often leads to insecurity. This is a self-perpetuating cycle we can all find ourselves in or are subjected to. It never leads anywhere else but in a downward spiral, as our egos keep us looking outward at others rather than working on our own shortcomings.

From your ego's perspective, a fault exists only outside of yourself. But from the point of awareness, we must appreciate that fault-finding in others indicates that there is an inherent flaw our ego is trying to mask. So how do we get around this, and how can we use it to our advantage when our ego is going to be wrestling with us to stay in this state of fault-finding?

The key to this is that before we work on our success, we must build our ego strength and have some core-guiding factors that we rely on over our egos' attempts at looking outwards. The more sure we are about *who* we are, the quicker we can build our ego strength and resilience to internal and external factors. And this all starts with our core values.

Core values are what I refer to as my "non-negotiables" and we teach them at length in our communities, because until we have these nailed there is no point in beginning to build anything. Imagine building a house without putting a solid foundation in. At the first sign of adverse weather, the building would likely crumble and fall, which is exactly what will happen as we begin to climb the ladder of success. We teach this within our communities before covering any money-making tactics or business strategy, because if you want to build entrepreneurial success that supports your lifestyle and aspirations, these need to be firmly considered.

What Are Core Values and How Do You Set Them?

As the phrase suggests, they are the values you hold at your core that guide you and keep you on the correct path. They are created to hold you accountable to your inner beliefs and wants, when the world around us tries to influence and pull it in other directions. Some people have one core value, others have multiple, and there is no right or wrong amount.

Core values can also be changed and adapted, added to or subtracted from as you grow on your journey through life. So don't be fearful of picking the right or wrong ones in this process. Just go with what feels right to you in your current reality.

As I write this book, I am a husband and father of two, and I believe I am a good person. This is reflected in the values I have lived by for the last decade, which are:

- **Family first**

  Above anything, my family and close friends have my focus and nothing will draw me away from them when they need me.

- **Healthy head and heart**

  If I am not fit and healthy, I will not be able to give myself to others or be in a position to build on where I am today.

- **Ethically earn**

  I make sure the value I provide outweighs the financial compensation. I do the right thing regardless of wealth.

- **Be silly, be honest, be kind**

  I don't take life too seriously. Life is a game and we should enjoy it!

These have steered me well and they all came from careful consideration about who I wanted to be and how I wanted to be perceived in the world. Sometimes they are not the easiest to live by, and at other times I feel completely in flow with them. The important thing is that they are my grounding point and they keep me accountable.

To create your own non-negotiables, the first thing you need to do is give yourself a little bit of time for self-reflection while treating the task with the same level of importance as the others that will lead you to success. This dedicated time will be used to think about what is most important to you and the type of person you want to be. It can be tricky to get the headspace to do this in your normal day-to-day life, so a good place to start is to take yourself off to a place that you find relaxing, like a cafe, spa or park, where ever you feel you won't be distracted so you can focus on this two-step process to identifying your non-negotiables.

Your PUSH and PULL List

Michael Jackson the wrote song *Man in the Mirror*, and the lyrics of the chorus are:

> *I'm starting with the man in the mirror*
> *I'm asking him to change his ways*
> *And no message could have been any clearer*
> *If you want to make the world a better place*
> *Take a look at yourself and then make a change*

Michael produced the song to show that if we want to change the way the world operates, then we all need to start by looking within and making personal changes. This is because we are ultimately the ones who are contributing to the overall problems the world faces. This is what stage one is all about, looking at the person staring back at us, to see if their actions and mentalities match those of the person we want to become.

We need to look deep inside of ourselves to understand if our actions and thoughts serve our new path and the new version of ourselves. And if not, how can we avoid being that person in the future? This process can take time, but the result is worth the work. It will allow your actions to multiply your progress as you move towards your version of success. To do this we are going to make a pull and a push list.

The Push List

The push list is everything you do in life that pushes you in the right direction. Whether it follows your morals, boosts your energy, makes you feel in flow or simply makes you happy, this list is going to be everything that you feel is working well for you and that you are going to maintain in your life. It can also be things you want to do more of. Here are some examples to get your creative juices flowing:

- Waking up rested and full of energy
- Appreciating the small things

- Giving back to my community

- Supporting those I care about

- Doing the right thing

- Putting myself first

- Making a difference

- Self-care

- Healthy body, healthy mind

- Exercising daily

The list can be as long as you like, as long as it is filled with things that genuinely work for *you*. This list should put a smile on your face, and if you were to add every part of it to your day, week or month, you would be having the time of your life. There will be elements that you already do, elements you wish you did more of and some that you have never done before but aspire to do.

The Pull List

The pull list is the direct opposite. Instead of writing things you do now that *are* working, this list will be made up of the things actively holding you back in your journey. These are all the traits, feelings and actions that have previously held you back that you are ready to stop doing. Some of these can include:

- Eating junk food

- Not prioritising health

- Living the highlight reel on social media

- Never saving money

- Not believing in myself

- Worrying about what others think

- Pushing those who help away

- Envious of others' success

- Overworking

The pull list is usually harder to write because we really have to focus on the "man in the mirror" and pull out all of the faults we know are damaging. The examples I have shared are generic but common, and there are likely some on the lists you will be able to resonate with.

Start there and build out your lists until you feel they are a good representation of who you want to be (push) and who makes up your current reflection (pull).

Productise to Prioritise

Now you have your lists, it's time to start looking for themes that appear in both of your lists, that can be married up and can become the base of your non-negotiables. Below are our two lists, with an example of where the two sides can be in conflict against each other so they can be put together:

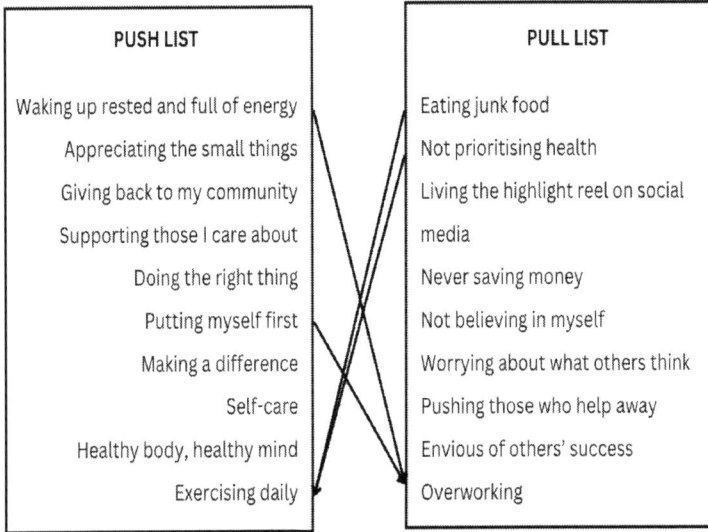

PUSH LIST	PULL LIST
Waking up rested and full of energy	Eating junk food
Appreciating the small things	Not prioritising health
Giving back to my community	Living the highlight reel on social
Supporting those I care about	media
Doing the right thing	Never saving money
Putting myself first	Not believing in myself
Making a difference	Worrying about what others think
Self-care	Pushing those who help away
Healthy body, healthy mind	Envious of others' success
Exercising daily	Overworking

Overworking can directly affect our ability to get proper rest and it is certainly not putting ourselves first. Similarly, eating junk food and not prioritising your health can be in part overcome by eating well and exercising. As you begin to marry these sides up, you will start to see common themes of what your non-negotiables need to become to change your mirror's reflection.

This exercise will give you the buckets that will make up your non-negotiables, but to make them memorable, we need to give them something you can visualise clearly and convey to people with ease. This is where we need to productise each group that we have created into something simple to remember.

Below I have listed some examples (some used to be my own non-negotiables) to help you get started.

If two of your items are more of "waking up with energy," and less of "running yourself until exhaustion from overworking," one of your non-negotiables might be:

> *"Put on your own oxygen mask first: Before I help others, I will ensure I am safe and well enough too."*

This was one of my blind spots until a mentor pointed it out. The idea of "putting on your own gas mask first" in a plane safety announcement (i.e. looking after yourself) serves as a reminder that I couldn't help others if I wasn't taking care of myself first. So, I would always pause to ensure I was okay before giving more energy to others.

> *"Food is fuel: The right fuel helps me win the race. If I put junk in, I should expect junk out. Eighty percent of the fuel has to be premium unleaded."*

I believe this non-negotiable could be applicable to most people. Food in the modern day is seen much more as an experience and source of entertainment than a source of fuel. It's tempting to always eat food that we see as "enjoyable" rather than picking what our body needs. I still live by this one today, although sometimes the 80% rule slips when the social calendar is in full flow. I still try to reign it back in because I know I perform at my best when I have the right fuel onboard.

The easier you make the "productised" version, the easier it will be to remember. This means you are more likely to actually prioritise it in your day-to-day life and be able to communicate to others what you are doing. Things like "spending more quality time with my family" can be shortened to something as simple as "family first," or "giving back to my community" could be "reinforcing roots."

Create as many of these non-negotiables as you want, and if you are struggling, just aim to create your first one. However, be sure that your non-negotiable is something you feel needs to be at the core of everything you do (remember these are the new foundations of our success). The only advice I would give is that sometimes less is more, and if you can have a handful or less of really well-considered values, you can set yourself up for huge success.

Once you have decided on your values, you want to lock them in and begin to practise adding them to your daily decision-making. There are loads of tips and tricks online about how you can print them and have them displayed somewhere you will see them constantly, or how you should recite them to yourself every morning like affirmations. I do none of this, I just make sure that my overall decisions are guided by them. Usually, you'll know when a decision isn't in line with your non-negotiables because something in your gut feels uneasy or wrong; that's when you can check back in on them to determine the right course of action.

There might also be some values that you aspire to live up to, but it is not the right time to implement them. These will be the ones where they are more the person you want to become rather than the person you are now, or where living by them would put you at a disadvantage rather than bringing positivity. It's 100% fine to create these, just keep them noted somewhere until they become a realistic value to implement. For me one of these values is:

> *"Bring real change to the world: Create positive change for as many people as I can, for as many generations as possible."*

For me to try and live this value now will only see me fail, as I have so much more I need to do personally before I can fully commit to this. I might never reach the point where it's possible, but by having the thought stored away, I'm confident my ideas will become reality and I will be able to achieve them. If I am unable to, so be it. At least I have a future version of myself that I aspire to be.

So, as we near the end of this chapter, you might be wondering: What is the secret to understanding real success? We have covered how success can feel, how others can influence it and, without the solid foundations of non-negotiables (values), how it's hard to truly build our future successful life. But we have yet to discuss what real success looks like. Unfortunately, you're going to have to wait a few more pages, because before we do, there is one more thing we need to look at: perfection.

Perfection can be a dangerous achievement to aim for and for those who do pursue it, you should approach with caution. Although perfection might be something we strive for, it can steal a lot from us in the process, including the elusive success we are looking for. This isn't always the case, and for some it might be the only way they can complete their journey to overall success. But for the most part we often miss out on the feeling of accomplishment and success because we never quite reach the perfection we strive for.

We will all have different tolerances for the term "finished." The best examples I can give to show the two ends of the spectrum would be:

1.) a composer trying to finish their life's work with the perfect composition of songs, with each note being the optimum pitch, frequency and volume; and

2.) a child who has been asked to wash the dishes.

One's version is finished after 10,000 hours of learning and honing a craft that could have spanned decades. The other is the quickest route to the finish line, leaving semi-washed dishes still strewn with food smudges on the draining board. Both will leave feeling satisfied with a job well done, but one clearly has higher standards for the finished article than the other.

Make sure you know where your standards sit in the spectrum of "finished," and understand that if you want to be successful, you should be shooting for somewhere a few leaps above the average and at least a few notches away from perfection. If your standards and aspirations are too low, you might never push hard enough to achieve the levels of success that are within your grasp. Too high and you might miss the point of doing it all in the first place, missing opportunities that are presented to you while you are too focused on that perfect crescendo.

Only now with these understandings and the foundations beginning to form beneath our feet can we truly begin to focus on what real success looks like, how it feels, what it means and how it will present itself to us. I have drawn a picture of it below:

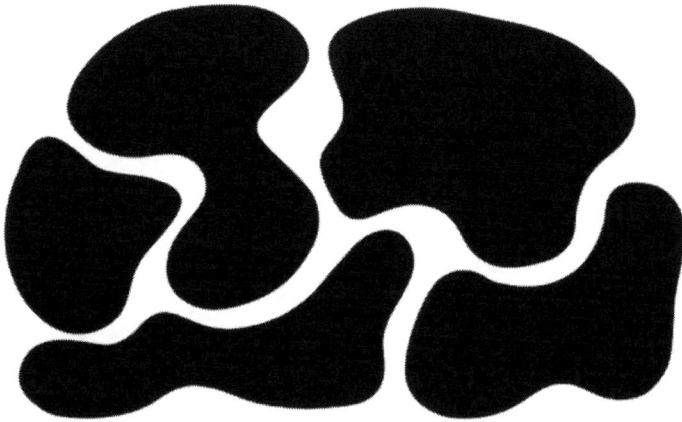

Do you now see how this whole chapter has been building to the above reveal of your success and how each part of the image above represents it? Can you feel how it instantly resonates with you and your core values? Of course, you can't, because it's just a picture of some blobs on a page and has sod-all to do with your success and how it might look. The reason? I haven't got the foggiest idea of how your success will look or feel, but what I *can* do is teach you how to visualise it for yourself.

Real success is different for every single person! Every individual reading this book will have their own version of success stored deep inside them. We just need to prize it out and put it in terms we can work towards. When we think about success, we usually only consider it to be the end goal for a task or process, like cooking a meal for friends or family. When it comes to overall success, we put very little thought or planning into it, we almost just "arrive" at the destination. The problem with this is if we reach the top of a ladder that we have spent a long time climbing, and it is up against the wrong wall, we will ultimately be disappointed.

For the remainder of this chapter, we will look at how we can better understand what makes us feel successful – which will help us in our journey later on. To understand what will make us successful, I want us to revisit the points of the Health, Wealth and Happiness Triangle. This time, let's not focus on where we are right now, but instead allow ourselves to envision where we want these parts of our lives to lead to. Stood where you are right now, how would you like these areas of your life to grow in the future to make you feel like what you are doing has been a success? Allow yourself to dream a little: Envision where you might end up if you align everything in your life towards these things, and start to imagine how it would feel once you are there.

As you do this, remember what we have learnt from previous chapters, and try to avoid the things that you would think others would want for you. Instead, focus only on what would make *you* feel happy, healthy and wealthy, as ultimately these are what should dictate how successful you are and feel. What has held you back previously will no longer be able to shackle these dreams. You can use your new understanding of your past, picking only the things that drive and serve you and casting out the old thoughts that held you back. Ignore the drives of sex and status and instead only focus on the individual pillars of health, wealth and happiness.

Some of the things you list might be things you are already achieving, and if they are, you can celebrate that you have found success accomplishing them. The others on the list might be a little way on the journey yet, which is also fine, as you can enjoy the journey to achieving them.

Health will look very different for all of us and it will depend vastly on our personality. I have an addiction to challenging and pushing myself, so I tend to set my fitness goals around pushing myself to be stronger or faster or have more stamina. Each time I accomplish a new milestone I appreciate and celebrate that level of success. You might have a personality that craves consistency or trying new things, so for you the goals will look very different to mine – and they *should*, because they are *your* version of your success in health.

The same can be said for wealth. Not everyone aspires to be financially wealthy. You might find your wealth in living from the land, or from helping others. Wealth can come in many forms, but the important factor is to understand what brings you wealth and where you are setting your sights to reach.

It will be no surprise that happiness follows in the footsteps of the other pillars, but happiness is likely the one where we can feel success in the quickest amount of time. When we truly understand what makes us happy, we can surround ourselves with it and embrace it in our successes. When we get really good at it, we can start to spread that happiness to others, which, in a bizarre way only returns greater happiness to the giver, and creates a sense of even greater success and reward.

This list should be enjoyable to write. If it is, you know it will be even more fun to pursue. It is *that* spark that is the start of real success. It's not being featured on the front of a magazine or an accolade that's bestowed upon you. These things might be milestones in the journey, but real success is comprised of the feelings and purposes we follow along that journey. The best thing is that these feelings are not designed to be enjoyed by others (although that might be a nice by-product). They are our own selfish views that cannot be changed by others.

You might now be thinking about our success from the vision of others, or how you'll need people to validate our accomplishments. That's your drive for sex and status speaking. Even with the validations, it would not make your success any more real or enjoyable. Real success only exists in our own minds, and it is built of the things we believe to be the most important to us.

To prove this, think about it from this perspective:

There will also always be people who view you as unsuccessful because their ego strength is low and they will only find fault in your position to protect them from their own shortcomings. You may know them personally or not at all, but their view has less to do with you and more to do with their own insecurities.

At the same time, there will also be people who view you as successful even if you don't feel it yourself. This will likely not be known to you but there will be people who either know you personally or via social media content who view your journey so far as successful. The success they see in you might align to your own vision or it could be a part of you that aligns to their own.

There are always going to be people who view you as successful or unsuccessful, maybe some who see you as a failure. But their opinion only exists within their reality and actually has little to no bearing on our own. Real success lies in the ability to create our own path and celebrate the milestones we manage to reach and learn from the ones that still evade us. If you improve by 1% each day, the successes you have created for health, wealth and happiness will soon be a reality, and you will either be enjoying the fruits they bring or making plans to travel to the next level of your own success.

There is one last thing to remember as you go on this journey, and it is another trap we all fall into, which, like our ego, can pull us back into a place of unhappiness and distract us from our journey. It's something that's driven by our sex and status drive and, with access to so many people across the world through social media platforms and online access, it affects so many of us on a day-to-day basis.

It is summed up in a saying by Theodore Roosevelt:

"Comparison is the thief of joy."

If we are to be truly successful, we must learn to ignore others' views of our achievements and avoid comparing these accomplishments with others'. Remember that real success is as individual as we are, so when you find yourself comparing with others, keep in mind that your drivers, values and reasons will differ greatly from theirs. No meaningful comparison can be drawn. Instead, fight the urge to judge status and celebrate others' achievements with them, because what's the point of the journey if we don't rejoice when others reach their milestones?

In the next chapter, we will look at how we can build on what we have created in this one, and dramatically accelerate our journey towards our own real success with just one simple life hack.

CHAPTER 6
SANITY AND VANITY

We previously explored how sex and status decisions are hardwired into us from birth, and how, as a species, they have driven us to achieve bigger and better things. At our core, these are still the default reasons we make decisions. But as the world around us has adapted, modern society has brought changes to the way we operate on a day-to-day basis.

This has introduced a new layer of decision-making that, although it has likely always been a factor, has recently escalated to a point where it now affects our daily choices. If left unchecked, it can derail a journey to success before it's even begun. That layer I'm referring to is whether a decision is one of *sanity* or *vanity*.

With years of population growth came the need for larger communities, pushing property to be built in closer proximity, which in turn naturally decreased our available privacy. On modern new-build housing estates in the UK, it is now commonplace to see rows of terrace houses, with interlocking gardens and driveways that all overlook each other. This layout maximises the efficiencies of the build and aims to make the most profit per square metre possible. This is not a bad thing. Communities are born in these environments, which can flourish and create beautiful friendships and support networks for those who live within them. It does, however, lead to competition amongst us, with the "status" drive taking the driver's seat. For example, it shows up as people wanting to park the best cars on their drive, to have the best-presented property or the biggest in the street.

The term "keeping up with the Joneses" is a common British phrase which dates back to a comic strip created by Arthur R. "Pop" Momand in 1913. It's an expression that means to live beyond your means in order to appear richer than you actually are.

Between technology advancements and the human need for connections, the want to be seen out-achieving our "neighbours" has accelerated drastically. We have been drawn into a world that has a constant lens focused on us both professionally and personally – and not just on a local scale, but a global one!

The terms follow, subscribe, like, comment, share, etc. are all embedded in our day-to-day language and are now the norm for 99% of us. Access to our lives is not just granted but has become a sought-after commodity, with many striving to gain more followers and traction across all social media apps and platforms.

The drivers for this can be both sex and status. Either way, access to our lives and what we fill them with is laid bare for the world to see, and that can lead us into a spiral of consumption to keep up the "highlight reel" that we share with the world. To really experience this, take your phone out and head to your go-to social media platform. Spend 60 seconds scrolling through the posts it presents, taking note of what they are filled with and what people are telling you about them. Everyone's social media will be different, with varying interests, but I'm willing to bet there is a common theme of people showing just how great they are at whatever they are displaying. Whether it be the meal they went out for, the experience they had, how hard they worked out at the gym or how early they got up to do it. Sound familiar?

Also, look at how much time you actually spent looking: Was it 60 seconds or did you get sucked into the social media world of peering into the highlight reels of others' lives? Look back on your own posts and ask yourself why you posted them. Was it for you? Or was it put there to show others a level of status or to attract others to you?

At this point, I just want to clarify that I am not against social media or showing people the good things that are in our lives. It is a part of modern society and I both partake and enjoy social media to a certain extent. It serves its purpose and, used in the right ways, can be a good addition to our lives. What this chapter focuses on is also not how we display our lives for others to see. That is a deeply personal part of our make-up and I would not want people to change how they go about this. Instead, by the end of this chapter, you will be able to tune in to your primal urges of sex and status to make sure the decisions they are driving serve you in the best way possible.

Imagine the benefit of knowing before you make a decision whether the outcome will advance your goals and accelerate your dreams, or if it might actually hinder your results – even if, in the moment, it feels like the right thing to do. Do you think this might be a worthwhile practice to implement in your life? Of all of the things I have done in my life to become successful, I would say this one bio hack has sped up the process the most. The best thing? It is also the simplest to adopt.

To understand why this is so impactful, we first have to understand the psychology behind why we make some decisions, and the natural reasoning our brain puts in place when we are weighing up our options. For most of us, this is felt more in the big decisions we are making. So the example I'll use won't be something we do daily, although this still applies to those decisions as well (but they will take a lot less time and likely happen in our subconscious minds).

Think of when we are purchasing a new phone. The likelihood is that a majority of readers will have done this at some point in their lives. Although a phone may appear to be a smaller purchase, when we change our perspective to the monthly contract costs and look at when a device is purchased upfront, it can cost in excess of £1,000, which to most is still a large outlay. The first thing to understand is that your sex and status drive is already at a disadvantage even before you explore the options. This is because companies selling the devices are absolutely incredible at marketing. They know how to tap into your deepest desires and create a sense of need and buzz around their products. They are intentionally searching for connections with your internal desires and they are phenomenal at connecting with them on a large scale. So from the outset, you are going to struggle with wanting the latest model on the market, with all the new shiny features they are promoting to enhance your life and experience. The company will show you just how amazing your life will look once you have committed to the purchase, listing off all the amazing photos and experiences you will have while clutching the new device in your hands, surrounded by your friends and family.

When we apply logic to advertising techniques, we know the tricks and games. We know that buying the latest model doesn't mean we are going to become amazing at snowboarding or shoot that movie-style shot while we are out and about. In all honesty, the activity shown in the ad is usually not something we would do at all, even if we had the best phone on the market. So why is it that we are drawn in? Why won't logic allow us to see past the glitz and the glamour? It's because we don't lead with logic; we lead with our hearts and the desires it gives us.

Logic goes out the window when we are presented with the option to buy, with our hearts taking over and leading our brains to think emotionally. We start to apply confirmation bias to the idea of the purchase, finding all the right reasons that we *should* commit to the 58-month contract for only £87 per month, rather than seeing the pitfalls that might come from it. For those who don't know what confirmation bias is:

Confirmation bias, n. The tendency to search for, interpret, favour and recall information in a way that confirms or supports one's prior beliefs or values.

Think back to the last significant purchase you made and recall the conversations you had with people when you were trying to make your decision. Did you start the conversation by telling them all the reasons you shouldn't buy? Or did you start by talking them through all the benefits you might have in your life if you move forwards and commit to the purchase?

For the most part, the people we share these purchases with are usually those whose opinions we value and trust, as we do want an honest answer from them. However, we often only share the information that supports our decision or confirms we're doing the right thing. Sometimes, these people will challenge us and ask more questions, which gives us the chance to either reconsider our decision or persuade them that their concern isn't a strong enough reason to hold back.

This goes even deeper. When the drive for sex or status is at its peak, we might subconsciously take confirmation bias to the next level. To understand if this is the case, ask yourself these questions:

The people you shared the decision-making process with, were they likely to agree that it was a good purchase?

Did you avoid telling people in your trusted network who you *know* would disagree with the purchase?

Did you avoid telling anyone altogether?

Did you realign the purchase to your core values and needs?

If the answer is "yes" to some or all of these questions, then you likely decided to buy before you even spoke with anyone. The reason you were asking people was more about validating your decision to purchase rather than genuinely considering if you were going to buy it in the first place. This doesn't just stop with purchases either. This can apply to all of the decisions we make regardless of if they are financial or not.

So if we understand how we naturally try to make decisions, how can we bio-hack ourselves into thinking differently? How can we ensure we don't allow our hearts to run wild while listening to the sex and status urge? To do that, we need to regain control by bringing logic into play.

Whenever I am facing a big decision financially, personally or in business, before I even consider the full details and let my heart engage in the process I use the Sanity or Vanity Scale to truly understand if it is the right move to make. This is the first of three tools I will share with you in this chapter. This tool has probably made me more money than it has saved me, because each time I use it, it keeps me true to my values, my position and the needs of my business and family. Although the method is not complicated, it is not an easy tool to use. It can only be 100% effective when we can be completely truthful with ourselves about the decision-making process, ignoring all confirmation biases pulling at our heartstrings.

So before we dive into the tool itself, let's look at what I mean by sanity and vanity in the context of these decisions.

Sanity

In order for the decision to be 100% sanity, it needs to have results that have *only* a positive impact on our current situation and that serve you in some way, financially or otherwise. With the same virtue, the decisions should have no negative downsides to our current situation. However, it can have a negative impact on future growth as long as the benefits to our current situation outweigh those future drawbacks. This might be tricky to wrap your head around so I have included an example below to help articulate it:

Option 1: Do nothing.

Option 2: Purchase an electric car:

- Monthly outgoings: £450

- Monthly savings on fuel: £150

- Monthly savings in company tax: £200

If we were to not take the above decision to move forward, the negative impact is not getting the company monthly savings of £350 on both tax and fuel. The next cost to the company is still £100 after these are considered and, if we were to choose option one, there is zero cost. So, looking at this limited information from just a finance perspective, the sanity decision would still be option 1: to do nothing.

Vanity

On the other end of the scale is vanity, which plays more into the sex and status camp for ways of thinking. A vanity decision is more about how you will be seen after making it, rather than the results it will give you. You are essentially focused on how the decision will make you appear to others, rather than on how it will truly benefit you.

Other than an increase in status or sex appeal, you will mostly see downsides from the decision in other areas, which will likely add pressure to that part of your life. I have included an example for this as well:

Purchase: New designer shoes that cost 40% of your monthly income

Outward Outcome: Social media posts, being seen in them, comments on your appearance and the perception of wealth and being able to "afford" such luxuries

Inward Outcome: Applying more budget pressures to afford the purchase, using credit for the purchase to spread the cost, which in turn applies pressure to monthly finances over a longer period of time

Both decision types can serve their purpose, and there is always space for both to exist. Sometimes, we will have to make sanity decisions when we want to make vanity, and at times we will make vanity decisions to help manage our overall sanity. What's important to remember is that the sum of all these decisions will shape our long-term success and influence how quickly we achieve it.

There's also a way to turn what seems like a vanity decision into a sanity-focused one by applying the 10% rule, which I'll talk about shortly. There's also a way to balance both worlds with decisions that land squarely in the middle, which can be explained with the tool below, the Sanity Vanity Scale:

Sanity	Vanity
10	10
9	9
8	8
7	7
6	6
5	5
4	4
3	3
2	2
1	1

I made this scale not only for my big decisions in business and life but also for the small daily decisions as they compound upwards over time. This tool has been, by far, the biggest contributor to accelerating my success. Without it, I believe my achievements over the past decade would have taken at least 30 years. In this part of the chapter, I'm not only going to explain how it works, but I am going to give you the one hack to use it effectively that will unlock your accelerated growth too.

First, the scale itself. At each end of the scale, you have the two extremes for sanity and vanity, which both score 10. They both have a sliding scale from 10 down to 1, and each side will be allocated a score. Where a decision has equal parts sanity and vanity, the score for both will be the same on each side and will be called a neutral decision, where both sides cancel each other out. This will be a balanced decision, and an example for that would be purchasing a sports car (vanity) that sits well within or below your monthly budget (sanity).

So, when scoring each decision against the scale, we first need to assess it honestly, without the usual confirmation bias we all tend to have. I do this intuitively, using my gut feel, but to help you get started before you develop your own method, I have provided a way for you to score each decision. You can also download and print this tool for use at www.lifestyle-entrepreneur.co.uk/stp.

The decision you are making:

_____

Score Scale:

0 – No

1 – Partially

2 – Yes

Sanity	
Can you afford this without any adverse effect on your budget?	0-2
Is this decision inward-facing?	
Does this decision serve you?	
Would the person most likely to disagree think this is a good choice?	
Do you NEED this to progress your current situation?	
Total Score:	

Vanity	
Will this purchase push you over budget?	0-2
Is this decision outward-facing?	
Does this decision serve others?	
Would the person most likely to disagree think this is a bad choice?	
Is this decision more of a WANT than a NEED?	
Total Score:	

The first section is for sanity, and the second section is for vanity, with each section having five questions. You will score each question and tally it up. Once you have the totals, you should now have a score out of 10 for both, which can be plotted on the Sanity Vanity Scale. You will now have a clear visual view of why this decision is being made. Below I have given a visual representations of the example of purchasing the designer shoes for 40% of your monthly income:

Sanity	
Can you afford this without any adverse effect on your budget?	0
Is this decision inward-facing?	0
Does this decision serve you?	1
Would the person most likely to disagree think this is a good choice?	0
Do you NEED this to progress your current situation?	0
Total Score:	1

Vanity	
Will this purchase push you over budget?	2
Is this decision outward-facing?	1
Does this decision serve others?	2
Would the person most likely to disagree think this is a bad choice?	2
Is this decision more of a WANT than a NEED?	2
Total Score:	9

Sanity	Vanity
10	10
9	9
8	8
7	7
6	6
5	5
4	4
3	3
2	2
1	1

So now that you know how to determine a sanity or vanity decision, this is the hack you are going to need to use if you want to accelerate your journey to success.

Like everything else when it comes to being successful, it's simple enough to understand but tricky to implement and follow. But I promise that if you do this consistently enough, it will have a huge factor in the time it takes to reach your first levels of success.

Delayed Gratification

When you are first pursuing your goals, every decision you make is going to be crucial, as you have very little momentum or longevity to play with.

Therefore, you're going to need to carefully choose the options that truly benefit you. For the first few months – or even years, if you are deeply committed – every decision should be a SANITY decision. It sounds simple, right?

It might be simple in principle, but when it comes to practising this, it becomes slightly more challenging.

When weighing up all our decisions, rejecting all that serve vanity and choosing those that serve sanity, it can seem pretty boring. Sanity choices don't tend to be the sexiest or the most exciting, but they are usually the ones that keep nudging us forwards towards our goals.

It is this art of delayed gratification that is the secret hack to rapid success. The ability to slow down the rewards to make way for the building blocks of success is what really makes the difference.

It is also the second tool in this chapter and the one that will give you the most success while applying the rules of sanity and vanity.

It might not fit the modern-day Instagram highlight reel, or give you bragging rights amongst friends and peers, but I promise that delaying gratification will see you overtake and exceed the majority of others to a point they could only dream of.

I practised delaying gratification for years, driving run-down cars, living in houses that were just big enough for our needs, wearing non-designer clothes and only throwing away socks when the holes were big enough to resemble a tunnel!

Even now, I still delay gratification and live well within my means to keep pushing the boundaries of my own success.

We do live a fantastic life and have access to some pretty fantastic things, but it sits well within our means, and we have a comfortable safety net and war chests at our disposal.

How do we still maintain this now, even when we do have some of the finer things in life? This is where the final tool of this chapter comes into play: the 10%

Rule. It is the tool you will be able to use to ensure that you keep a check on the decisions you make and that you have a balance in your decisions to keep you on the path to success at all times.

The 10% Rule

The 10% rule is something I put in place to allow me to dream big with the vanity choices but only act on them at the right time. This only became apparent to me quite a long way into my journey to success.

I had been practising delayed gratification and using the Sanity or Vanity Scale for a number of years, with my sole focus being on sanity decisions, to the point where I became quite bored. It was only when I realised some of the vanity dreams I had been having years ago were no longer vanity decisions; instead with my new position in success and financial freedom, they had become sanity ones.

This is where the 10% rule was born, and this is how it can work for you. In the early days of your journey or in your new pursuit of success, when you come across decisions that sit on the vanity side of the scale, make a note of them and "save" them for later.

As you climb the ladder of success, from time to time bring out these decisions for reassessment, taking your new position and circumstances into account.

At the point you are able to score your previous vanity decision, at only 10% vanity and 90% sanity (1/10 and 9/10), you can seize the moment.

Make that previously passed-upon vanity decision, having delayed gratification in lieu of accelerated growth and success, and enjoy every single moment of it!

These moments feel like magic, as you have all of the enjoyment with none of the remorse.

Delaying gratification will take time to commit to, and there is a personal balance you will find, which will change and adapt as you traverse your own journey. Sometimes it will be easy to stick to and other times it will feel like the worst thing to be doing.

The thing to remember is that, by compounding the good decisions, you will move in the right direction and reach your version of success faster by choosing only those decisions that benefit you.

In the next chapter, we will explore the importance of a well-programmed internal sat-nav, understand where we want ours to be pointing, and examine how the anti-climax of arriving at our destination can throw us off course.

CHAPTER 7
YOUR PERSONAL SUCCESS SAT-NAV

Imagine moving away from home and setting up a new life somewhere else, leaving everything you knew behind. Now, imagine doing that with zero knowledge or prior thought to the type of new life you would want to live. Or imagine physically walking out of your front door and not even knowing what direction you should start walking in.

Although this would be one hell of an adventure, it's leaving *a lot* to chance. What will you encounter on the journey? What areas will you pass through? Will you meet good or bad people? How long will it take to get there, and ultimately, what will the destination look like? There are likely people that would class these conditions as ideal, but I would hazard a guess that these people are few and far between.

So if the idea of leaving home to start a new life with no plan sounds bizarre, why do so many of us move through time without a pre-programmed destination? Why do we allow life to make our decisions for us rather than take action to secure our own destiny? I was one of these people, so I know the familiar feeling of allowing life to take its course and living with the results that can come from it.

Now you might be sat thinking this doesn't sound like you. You might have had a career path and plan laid out that you are actively working towards, or have even achieved before reading this book, which is fantastic. The difference here would be: Have you created your path to success and your health, wealth and happiness freedom? Do you have the road map pre-programmed against these pillars, and are you certain of the date you will arrive?

By the end of this chapter, you will be able to dial in the coordinates of your Personal Success Sat-Nav. This is so that you can set the end goal well before you begin, and you are always pointing in the right direction with your non-negotiables considered. But before you do, I want to take you back to my old life and how things used to be, way before I started building the frameworks that you are learning in this book today, and before I found my success.

The year is 2007 and I'm a *very* different person to the man I am today. Back then, I was overweight, a smoker and thought I was the absolute mutt's nuts living in a two-bed flat (that we claimed was a three-bed because it had a reasonably large storage room that we converted) with three of my best mates, which I am nearly 100% sure was not legally rented due to the state the place was in. The electricity was supplied by a coin metre. (Remember the 20p sweet machines you used to get gumballs out of? Like that.) The metre constantly needed to be fed £1 coins to keep the lights and heating on. There was no gas, so we used storage heaters during the winter to try to stay warm. All I remember is, one year, the bathroom was so cold that the toilet water froze over, and we would boil a kettle to defrost it before use.

What 19-year-old cares about that, though? In my eyes, life was good. I was with my mates. I was having fun, and I was living off my own buck. I was working two jobs at the time: one as a forklift driver and the other as a chef in a local pub. I worked around 60 hours a week to fuel goings out on the weekends while still being able to afford to run the flat and my car. I had zero savings, zero education and – to be honest – zero plan.

I had fallen into kitchen work at the age of 16, training to be an à la carte chef in a local pub restaurant (under a fantastic mentor), and I likely chose this route as at one stage, both my Mum and my Dad had been in the catering industry. Given that my GCSE grades were not up to scratch, I didn't even attempt to apply for a uni place like my friends. Instead, I went out into the working world earlier than most and learnt how to graft for my money.

The warehouse job came through a friend who was working in the same warehouse. He recommended it as a good way to make money, so I applied and, to my surprise at the time, got the job. I used to work a 4-days-on and 4-days-off shift pattern, with work days spanning 12-hour shifts. I remember being depressed in the winter because I would start work before the sun rose and head home hours after it had set. The only time I would actually get to see or feel the sun on my skin was during my 30-minute lunch breaks, which I would spend huddled on a bench outside, chain-smoking cigarettes and chatting with the other people on shift.

Without a plan, I had no objectives in my life. I simply enjoyed the moments that I got to have fun with my mates, while in the other gaps, I earned money by providing my time to employers. Even though I had no savings, no prospects of saving or any idea how I would earn more money (because I had already used up all of my time), it didn't worry me because I thought this was all there was to life.

So what was I like as a person back then versus the person I am today? And what made the difference successful against the odds – as an uneducated, overweight, skinhead 19-year-old (oh yeah, I forgot to mention I shaved my head too because someone said I would look cool. I didn't…). To be honest, a lot of my characteristics were the same. What was different then were just the things I told myself and what I had thought it was that made me a successful person.

If you were to ask the 19-year-old me to describe myself, I would say:

"I have a great work ethic and I can get on with 99% of the people I meet. I have a good ability to get people to like me and my biggest aim in life is to make other people happy." (This is actually what I used as a child as my main ambition in life).

If you asked me what made me successful, I would tell you:

"If the people around me are happy and laughing, I am successful."

I used to focus so heavily on this and would rarely consider if I was actually happy within myself. This version of me carried on for many years, with the only changes being the job roles I took during that time.

In the five years I worked for the company where I started in the warehouse, I went from warehouse operative to forklift driver, from forklift driver to team leader, and then from team leader to logistics lead. Afterwards, I went on to be a key account manager for a £million+ client before becoming a deputy branch manager. The last position I took at the company was as a co-branch manager in a top London store, which was sought after as a role in the business. Did I aim for any of these jobs? No. They simply happened because I made the people I worked with like me and allowed my work ethic to speak for itself.

I used to make friends with everyone who worked in the building. I would find a way to connect with whoever I met on a higher level than just a "hi'" in the corridors of the building. Was this to make sure I could climb the ladder to corporate success? No, it was to fulfil my desire to make everyone's life around me better by giving them a little happiness and laughter. So without a pre-destination set, and with some levels of success in a short space of time, why wouldn't I just carry on as I was?

Honestly, I could have, and if I had, I imagine I'd be some level of area manager or perhaps a director by now, earning a good salary and likely on track to retire at around 70 years old. So why didn't I? For many years, I didn't even think about it. It dawned on me late into this journey that I was climbing a ladder to success, yet I hadn't picked the wall it was leant up against. The value the ladder offered me was money, and, towards the top, it felt good. The cost, however, was a lot greater, as it was taking my time away from me. This is something the majority of us will feel or have felt at some point – and not just those in the corporate world. Entrepreneurs also build businesses that are meant to give them time freedom, but those end up consuming their creator instead. All too often, it's only realised a long way into their journey.

After the realisation that I was moving forwards in the wrong direction, there was a change that I needed to make. I didn't have the confidence in my ability or intelligence to run a business of my own, but I could see the entrepreneurial journey was likely going to give me everything I desired, so I spent the next seven years working within tight-knit startups, again, working my way up the ladders. The first startup I worked for saw me running a property maintenance and customer service department until I eventually ended up as the general manager for the full UK business. The second I started back as a customer experience manager, I rose through the ranks to become a Global brand manager looking after the UK, USA, Europe, Australia and New Zealand.

These jobs allowed me the freedom to be one of the key persons of influence when the business was growing, without what I saw at the time as the risk of owning my own business. It also gave me the confidence to challenge my perceptions of being a business owner, and during my time at these businesses, I also started my own on the side, which ended up generating me more personally than my employed roles. All these, along with the guidance of mentors, showed me that I had been selling myself short for a long time and not recognising my true abilities.

I was lucky enough to find the paths that I did through a mixture of luck, opportunities and mentors holding mirrors up for me to look into, but it took me over 15 years to realise the potential I had and what I could do for myself. Would I change it? No, because I wouldn't have been able to build the tools and tactics I now rely on to be successful or share them with you in this book.

So, how can you start to program your Personal Success Sat-Nav and how can you choose the destination before you set off? As you can see from my journey, I was not always sure of where I was going. A lot of the time, I was not even tuned into the fact that I was travelling in the wrong direction at all. To ensure you don't do that, too – or to stop doing that if you already are – we are going to look at how you can align your version of success to your core values. Then we are going to plot out which wall your ladder needs to be leant up against to achieve your health, wealth and happiness goals, before you put your foot on the first rung.

From the previous chapters, you will have already spent some time considering what you want from your new life. It should begin forming a picture in your mind. The tricky part is figuring out the quickest route to getting there. I wish the next sentence was telling you to just punch in the postcode and follow the calming voice giving you the next direction to take. But the terrain of life is not quite the same as the A to Z maps of the UK, unfortunately (for those too young to have ever seen these, think Google Maps on paper!).

Instead of focusing on the route we should take, for this chapter, we are going to cover the tools we will use to *not* take the wrong turns in our journey. In other words, we need to find out which decisions we need to avoid making so that we get to the right place. This is similar to Sanity and Vanity in the sense that one choice pulls us closer, while the other will let us stagnate or push us away. However, it focuses more on ensuring we're facing the right direction when making the sanity decisions as they are presented.

Look over the push and pull lists you have put together previously and begin to focus on all the choices you would make about your career, business and personal life that *wouldn't* serve these lists. Where the lists were enjoyable to write and allowed us to be in a dream state, at this stage of our journey, we will be looking through them again with a cautious and protective mind's eye, allowing us to see all of the threats and risks that could derail our dreams.

What we are aiming to do here is gather information that will build our "stock trader rules," which is essentially a list of questions we can ask ourselves while we travel our path to success. This ensures the decisions we make are aligned with our goals rather than relying on optimism and "gut feel," which can be clouded by our own confirmation bias. These rules are going to link directly back to the Health, Wealth and Happiness Triangle to ensure we also remain balanced in our journey.

For each opposing risk we find for our push and pull lists, we are going to write a question that we will be able to measure our decisions against in the future. This will inevitably keep us on the correct path if we choose the right outcome.

Health

For health, if we had the ambition of being athletic and want to regularly attend and enjoy local fitness clubs to build up strength, stamina and connections, a risk to this would be in taking a career that meant lots of travel and time away from home. This wouldn't be impossible to manage, but it would take us out of the flow of our desires.

The question you would ask here is: Does this decision still allow me regular time to attend my fitness classes? If the answer is no, it's not the right decision.

Another example would be someone who'd like to spend time outdoors enjoying as much nature as possible to promote robust mental health. If you were to compromise and take a position in an office-style environment, no amount of ladder climbing is going to allow for this dream to be met.

So your question could be: Will I be able to spend 50% of my time working outdoors? Again, if the answer is no, it's not the right decision.

Wealth

For wealth, you might have put on your list the ability to earn enough money to have a 50% disposable income. This would not marry up to a personal decision to live in a property that leverages our position. It means you can only just afford the mortgage payments. It might also not be conducive to apply for multiple, high-limit credit cards, or buying items on credit.

Your question here would be: Does this decision allow me to keep 30% of my salary as savings? If the answer is no, it's not the right decision.

Can you see how these non-negotiable questions keep us aligned with our path? Now let's look at the same goal for wealth, but this time from a different perspective.

If we want to live with 50% of our income as disposable and a promotion comes around, that would see us increase our salary by 20%. On the surface, it will look great, but if we need to relocate to an area where the costs of living are going to increase by 25%, this may no longer look attractive.

The same question applies and the outcome would remain the same.

Happiness

If, like me, you want to spend more time with those you love and do the things you enjoy to increase your levels of happiness, it would not be an option to look at career paths that require more than 40 hours per week of your time or positions that have shift patterns due to the volatility they bring. When those roles come up, you could try to justify them as a short-term sacrifice and you could tell yourself: "I will have more time once I move up the ladder," but the harsh reality is we don't know how long we have on this earth. You are sacrificing your time *now*.

The question here would be: Does this decision take time away from my family and personal life? If the answer is yes, it's not the right decision.

Challenge every point on each list from as many personal and business perspectives as possible, and once you have exhausted all of the threats you can think of, put the list in priority order according to which could derail you the quickest or the most at any given time.

This will not be an exact science. As you move through your journey, you will need to edit, add and take away from the list, because we cannot predict what will happen over the coming months or years. However, what this list will do is give you a list of questions you can ask yourselves when those important decisions, moves and moments in life come up, so we can analyse each one to ensure it serves us best. These lists are going to be the basis of our stock trader rules.

Stock Trader Rules

Stock trader rules are a set of questions we can ask ourselves about any decision. Unless we have all of those questions answered in the correct way, we cannot take action.

I use stock trader rules in my personal life and our businesses to make sure that all of my decisions are aligned with the direction of the end goal.

We use the term "stock trader rules" as it mimics a technique used by the most successful currency, commodity and stock traders and has been developed for one very specific reason in mind: to trade with your head and not your heart.

We've all had those decisions put before us, where we *really* want to do something because it would fill our hearts to the brim. But we know deep down the decision makes no logical sense and that, really, we should not move forward. The best example I could give for this is purchasing a house.

When we view a house, sometimes it is the completely wrong one for our current position. It might need more work than we would like to be doing or cost too much. The garden might not be south-facing or it could be too far away from where we socialise or work, but once our hearts become attached it is so hard to see past its beauty or potential. They say all homes are bought with the heart, but smart purchases are found by the heart and negotiated with our heads.

Stock traders create a criteria list that ensures that when their heart (or gut) finds a trade they believe would make them money, they run it through the criteria on the list and make sure that all the boxes are checked. If some boxes can't be ticked, the trade doesn't happen (even if it's just one!). Ahead of time, this allows the trader to set out the rules by which they want to logically make their trades. It also prevents them from using gut instinct alone or with their hearts (i.e. emotionally charged decisions). They say the most successful traders are those who are able to trade on a completely emotionless basis, and the same applies to people in business.

Have you ever come across someone either personally or otherwise who has all the energy and ideas in the world, but they can never execute against them, or a person who always seems to have "bad luck"? Each time they have another new idea that they are determined to try, it's met with phrases like, "I have a really good feeling about this one," or "Luck will be on my side this time." Why do you think they fail? Is it because they failed to plan? Did they not create a robust model to follow our rules of engagement? Or perhaps both things combined amongst other reasons?

Imagine that football never existed, and the person who created it had the vision of it being played in every city in the world, having countries compete in international tournaments with players being traded between clubs for millions of dollars. Now, imagine that when they brought the idea to life, they didn't create any rules for the game or structure for the leagues. It would be chaos! People would love the concept, but the reality would fall very short. Unless the creator could identify, adapt and implement change quickly, people would lose interest, and the idea would die as quickly as it was conceived.

Your success is no different. Approaching it with no plan, no roadmap and no rules will likely have the same results. But this time, it will be you who loses interest when you see no progress or results.

So you are going to use the lists of questions you have created in this chapter to make stock trader rules that match the part of the journey you are on. This is to not only keep you making smart decisions but to also keep your focus on the end goal at all times and not allow your heart to trade you into reverse.

Your stock trader rules are going to be bucketed up into a smaller, more concise list that can be used to measure the viability of an idea or decision as opportunities present themselves. The list must be made up of rules that *cannot* be broken. To move forwards with the decisions, you must be able to confidently tick all of the rules off to ensure you stay on track.

Bucket up your questions that are similar and make one master question you can ask yourself when you need clarity on a decision. Once you have these master questions, review them against your non-negotiables. The ones that match your non-negotiables the most will be your stock trader rules; these will be the questions you ask yourself when you need to make a decision.

If one of your non-negotiables is "family first," your master question might be: Does this decision take me away from my family for more than one day a week?

Set what you are comfortable with, understanding that these are going to be the anchors that hold you true to your path when emotions are trying to sway your ship.

I have given an example below of someone whose idea of success is to be both time- and financially-free. Their core values consist of family first, love thy neighbour (i.e. being involved in supporting the community daily) and ethically earning.

They are currently working in a high-level corporate management position where they earn £80k per year pre-tax, of which they have 10% left at the end of each month that they attribute to savings. For the £80k salary, they are required to work 50 hours per week in the city of London, which is a 30-minute train journey each way (meaning their full committed time is roughly 55 hours per week).

For this example, let's assume their name is Sue.

These are their stock trader's rules for their next move:

- I must give less of my time but earn more.
- I must not work away from my family or community.
- I should exceed my current income by 20%.

- I should be in a more senior role in my new position.

The role above them in management is opening up in the same company they currently work for, and the position is posted to the company before being advertised externally. During a meeting with the company's board of directors, Sue's name is put forward as a potential candidate for the role with a strong chance of success if she were to apply. This information is given to her in her next one-to-one.

The role's details are as follows:

- Salary: £120,000 + expenses
- Working Hours: 40 hours per week, one week in office, one week remote
- Title: Senior Manager
- Location: Dubai

The business is opening up a new branch overseas and the role would be leading the project to establish the business in Dubai. This will require Sue to work in a shift pattern where she would travel to the U.A.E once a fortnight to work in the new business, with the following week being working remotely from her home. Sue feels this opportunity is a good fit for her initially as the extra money would help with her overall financial goals. Moreover, working fewer hours would be perfect. She would also be in a position where she would be the head of a new business, which is an exciting prospect.

Lets now check this against her stock trader rules:

- I must give less of my time but earn more. ✓

- I must not work away from my family or community. ✗

- I should exceed my current income by 20%. ✓

- I should be in a more senior role in my new position. ✓

We have ticked all but one of Sue's criteria, which is to not take a position that takes her away from her family or community. Sue wrote these stock trader's rules to ensure she sticks to her success path, and it was important to her that she remains in constant physical contact with her community as this is within her core values. This job ticks 75% of her stock trader rules and her heart is telling her to take the role. This is a position we will all find ourselves in at some point, ready to compromise on our plan because we find something that is nearly what we want and has some great criteria.

In this example, Sue sticks to the plan and does not apply for the job. Instead, her manager gets the role and heads up the new Dubai division, which is a lot more challenging than the company had expected, requiring the new leader to work three out of four weeks in the country to get the team where it needs to be, which eventually ends up leading to being in the country full-time (for which they are compensated with additional salary benefits). With this role filled, the UK team needed a new leader. Sue applied and became successful in her application, with her new role having the following details:

- Salary: £100,000 + Expenses
- Working Hours: 40 hours per week, 3 days in London office, 2 remote
- Title: Senior Manager
- Location: London.

Let's evaluate this one against Sue's stock trader rules:

- I must give less of my time but earn more. ✓
- I must not work away from my family or community. ✓
- I should exceed my current income by 20%. ✓

- I should be in a more senior role in my new position. ✓

This role ticks all of Sue's stock trader rules and moves her along her pre-planned success journey. All she had to do was trust the process and make the right decisions to stay on track.

Having stock trader rules for each part of your journey will keep you aligned to the path you are looking to take. Even when your heart feels like you are missing an opportunity that could get you there quicker, something new will show up to pull you up the ladder. Not every opportunity that presents itself is going to be the right opportunity for *you*. It's important to check against our rules to prevent our hearts from getting carried away in what could be a vanity decision that could ruin our sanity down the road.

The question remains though: How do we know which wall to place our ladder up against, and when does the ladder need to move? For this, we are going to dream big but plan bigger as we start to understand what it might take for us to get there.

So, as we begin, it's worth noting that no one will share exactly the same goals or aspirations. Some might be similar, but they will have their own differences based on our internal desires and core values. Given we all live in a world where time and money play a huge factor, these are the areas of the dreams we are going to focus our time on during the remainder of this chapter.

Take some time to think about where you see your success taking you and all the things that come with it. Make a list of them as they come to your mind and be as detailed as you can with how your new life looks, feels, where you are and who is with you. Explore things like what your house is like: its size, the area it's in, etc. Be specific and consider all the large aspects of your life that can be realised with success. This list might take you some time to create, but the more time you spend on it, the more likely it is you will achieve your overall goals and success. You can also add to this list over time, adapting it as your journey unfolds and new desires become important.

Once complete, it will look like you have created a shopping list for all of the things you need once you are there. Now all we need to do is figure out the cost to you!

I now want you to add to columns like in the example below (or a template for this can be found at http://www.lifestyle-entrepreneur.co.uk/stp.)

New Life Details	Money	Time
4-bedroom, detached		
Golf membership		
Premium car		
Weekly bike rides		
Etc.		

Next to each of your new life's details, I want you to estimate how much time and money you will need for this to become a reality. For some, you might not need to allocate any for either, but give some thought to those that need one, the other, or both.

New Life Details	Money	Time
4-bedroom, detached	£1500pm	0
Golf membership	£570pm	18 hours per month
Premium car	£600pm	0
Weekly bike rides	£0	3 hours
Etc.		

Once you have all your time and money costs allocated to each item, you will be able to make an estimate below the headline values (or costs) that you will need to live your new life. These might seem ridiculous or easily in reach; just stick with this process at this stage:

*(Use the best calculation period for you)

Money required per (*Year/Month/Week) for new life: £XXX

Free time required per (*Year/Month/Week) for new life: XXX Hours

Depending on your list, these numbers might be small, large, within close reach or seem impossible. All of these are fine. You can easily build a plan to achieve any of them. If your figures are achievable quickly and easily, I would challenge you to dream bigger. If your figures are astronomical and seem like a million miles away, then it's time we get to work on achieving some or all of them! Either way, you now know the money you will need for your new life and the free time you will need to enjoy it.

You might not be sure how we are going to achieve it yet, but you now have a target to aim for. And that is all we needed to achieve in this chapter. Your Personal Success

Sat-Nav has a destination (which you just worked out) and a way of avoiding the routes that will take us longer to reach our goals (your stock trader rules).

We will be revisiting these results throughout the book. We will start to not only program your destination but also look at how you can make these figures into a manageable and achievable plan, regardless of how large these numbers might feel right now.

CHAPTER 8
PREPARING FOR DEATH

For the last few chapters, we have been entirely focused on preparing for success. This includes understanding what the three pillars of success – Health, Wealth, and Happiness – mean to us, reviewing our past to challenge limiting perceptions and learning how our decisions are shaped and how listening to the wrong ones can hold us back. We've also explored how to find our path to success.

All the work you have done so far has led you to this part of your life: the present version. Imagine you are standing on the summit of a mountain that represents the life you have created thus far, and you have been looking back over the scenery you have created. With each chapter, you have understood more about the paths you have taken and what you want to do more and less of in your journey. You should be able to stand with an understanding of what got you here, and how you are going to use that knowledge to shape your new journey with a predetermined route and destination. If you turn 180°, leaving the well-studied and walked landscape behind you, you are now presented with the next mountain to climb, with a clearly marked summit. Using the knowledge from the last landscape, you are also able to plot out the best and fastest route to it. But as you study it, you notice the new route is a climb that you are not used to.

There are tricky traverses and inverted ledges that will prove to be challenging. The slopes are made of sharp edges and some have loose gravelly surfaces rather than the softer and more sturdy paths that you scaled in the last climb. You look down at your gloves, ropes and pulleys; although these helped you on your last ascent along with your existing climbing techniques, only some of them are going to be useful for the onward journey and the new challenges that it will present. At this point, we have two options: We either approach the climb and begin, hoping that we will succeed as we are, or we have to make some changes.

Like in the previous chapter, the tools, ropes and techniques that I am talking about symbolise all of the knowledge you've learnt about yourself that has led us here. If you continue to climb carrying all the parts of yourself that no longer serve you, it would be like carrying those tools and ropes in a bag on your back. It becomes a heavy burden that slows you down and saps your energy, eventually leading you down the old paths you used to walk – which is why you have to leave them behind before you start. By leaving them behind, you create a new version of yourself, one more equipped with the terrain ahead. The more you allow this new version of yourself to lead, the more likely the older, less experienced and less capable versions of yourself will be recognisable, to the point where, eventually, our old persona will die to make way for the new.

It is easy to say, "Wake up tomorrow and begin life as the new version of yourself," and I see this so often in self-help books, blogs and in the visioning mentality. But the realities of this change are so much harder to deal with. When I'm talking about the death of our old persona, I'm of course talking metaphorically. But you might be surprised at some rising elements of grief as you leave behind a version of yourself that you have known for so many years.

Grief is tough. So when death happens around us and to those we hold close and dear, we have to go through it because death in the real world is final. In this version, however, it would be very easy to revert to our previous version if we allow our ambitions to be defeated by the issues that the grief process throws up.

This is made harder again when we take into consideration that it is not just *you* who will be grieving the death of your old self. Those who know you well will also have to adapt to the loss of someone they might have known for decades to make way for the new way you have chosen to be. As you make changes, you will become vulnerable to critique from those around you, much like the lobster who sheds its old shell. It goes through a period of time that is easier for predators to attack, as its new shell is soft and supple. You will experience the same feeling of vulnerability as the new world adjusts to your new persona and outlook.

Depending on the changes needed, the new reborn version of yourself could be fundamentally different to the one those around us are used to. As the human default is to reject change and search for ways to bring back what we know, you might begin to feel the pressure to do so.

We cannot stop the grief process. So, in this chapter, we are going to focus on how we can best prepare ourselves and others for it. The better you prepare, the more likely it is you will have the best chance for success moving forwards. This is an important step in your journey as it is not just going to happen once, but many times in the span of your life if you want to advance to new levels of success. Sometimes, these changes will be minor and will blend into the background, like lighting a candle in a large room with only a few noticing the subtle differences. Others will be dramatic and will come with the heat and scale of a forest fire, which in our own circles will feel like it can be viewed from space.

An example that I can give of a large change event in the forest-fire end of the spectrum is something that is happening more and more as the world around us becomes more accepting of how we identify: when someone goes through a sex change. Whether physical, emotional or otherwise, if you are in a situation where you were born into the wrong body and have the bravery to share the real you with the world in all its glory, you will experience all seven stages of grief. Both you and those around you will have to go through the shedding of your old self.

The likelihood is that the person undergoing change will have experienced grief privately, possibly confiding in a few close and trusted loved ones they believe will be supportive. This exposes them to their own grief as well as that of others as the process unfolds. At some stage, however, they might choose to be publicly recognised in their new body; at this point, they must contend with the reactions and grief from the broader community.

A few years back, I was invited to a stag do by a friend, where a 50-strong ensemble of blokes was going to descend on Bournemouth for a weekend to celebrate the stag's last days of freedom, with the usual banter, activities and drink-fueled fun. During the planning stages, a WhatsApp group was created so we could all get to know each other, plan logistics and payments, and of course, find ways to embarrass the stag. While this was all going on, the stag had been removed from the group to ensure we were keeping the plans a surprise, but one of the members (whom we will call Gary) reached out to him saying he needed to chat.

The two had known each other for years, having gone to university together and have for 15 years since been playing football with the same group of lads from those days (about 25 of the stag do group were made up of these football / uni mates). They had countless memories of lads' banter, nights out chugging pints and games of Sunday league football, so as you can imagine they were all quite close. Gary had messaged the stag to make him aware that he might not be able to make the stag do and that he was sorry to miss out on it. Obviously, given the relationship they had, the stag questioned why he couldn't make it, as it would be a shame not to have all the lads together celebrating.

Gary then delivered the news that he was unable to attend because he was no longer "one of the lads" any more. In fact, over the last few months, he had begun his rebirth and was now known as Molly. Given the nature of a stag do and that traditionally it was only men who attended, Molly felt that although she had a long-lasting relationship with the stag, it would not be right for her to attend; it was only fair to let the stag know why. She then proceeded to inform the football WhatsApp group of the same news, fully committing to the death of Gary and the rebirth of Molly.

What do you think happened when she broke the news to the 25-strong, lad-fueled football WhatsApp group that Gary was no longer alive, and Molly was the new woman in town? Do you think they all re-adjusted their perception and memories from the last 15-plus years, filled them away and cracked on? Of course, they didn't. They all started journeys of grief for Gary, whom they had known and loved as a friend for all that time.

The great news is they are a wonderful bunch of lads, and while they managed their grief for Gary, they welcomed Molly with open arms and began making new memories with her, including the stag do, of which she became an integral part. Although the changes from Gary to Molly might be seen as "extreme" in this example, the changes you are going to make in your own rebirth could be received by those around you as fundamental to who you are, which is why you need to prepare for the "funeral" to manage any grief that is felt.

Some cultures believe that by putting items into a coffin or by surrounding ourselves with items in our place of burial or rest, we will take these things through the afterlife. You are going to go through something similar, but rather than material possessions, you are going to choose which parts of your inner self are going to be carried forward to the new version of you, and which parts are no longer serving you. Some of these might be small changes and others might be drastic. Either way, you are going to emerge on the other side as a newer and improved version of yourself tailored specifically towards your success.

This process can be enjoyable for us, as we get to completely reinvent who we are and what we believe to be true about ourselves and the world around us. It can also come with an equal measure of pain, as we have to leave parts of ourselves – which we might have been carrying around for an exceptionally long time – behind. This can be hard for everyone around us, so it's important to understand the pains grief brings, which are easily explained by looking at the seven stages we go through:

1. Shock

2. Denial

3. Anger

4. Bargaining

5. Depression

6. Testing

7. Acceptance

Of course, we are not really dead. We have just changed to a new version of ourselves, but this will still take some adjustment. The amount of adjustment will be proportional to the severity of the change we have made. An example of this would be Molly's journey to her first stag do versus if we change our hairstyle. One is going to have more adjustments for those around us.

The first thing to understand is the way others are feeling is very REAL to them and that they are entitled to go through this process. You cannot control it; you cannot remove it. But you *can* support them to hopefully allow them to understand and embrace your newest self. Some of the stages might be short while some might be long. Either way, you have to allow people to travel through them at their own pace.

Here's how some of these stages might look in reality:

Shock: People might not know what to say, how to act or how to be around you once you change. They might put distance between you and them, or they might openly tell you they just weren't expecting it to happen.

Denial: Comments like, "It's a phase," and "No chance this lasts long," come to mind (think of a pub-going man giving up drinking or a pack-a-day smoker quitting overnight). They might choose to ignore the changes and treat you as if nothing was different.

Anger: Anger can bring two things: confrontation or closed-door conversations. Both lead to upset. They might try to say things that make you feel bad: "You never come out anymore," "You're boring," or "You used to be so much fun."

Bargaining: When anger doesn't serve up results, bargaining usually ensues with pleas like, "Come on, it's just once," "For old times' sake, shall we just do it?" They want you to revert and assume you are not committed to the new version.

Depression: Depression comes in many forms, and I am not qualified to tell you how they might look. How they have appeared in my past are typically being ignored and arguments with tears; it sometimes looks similar to acceptance but without the air of support.

The first five stages are the hardest, with a lot of time being focused on resistance to the change. Meanwhile, the next two stages are when you can finally begin to be confident in the person you have become.

Testing: This is where peers will make attempts to move forwards and see how the new version of you and your relationship can fit into your life.

Acceptance: This is where we hope we will all get to, where the newest version of ourselves is accepted. It doesn't always mean previous relationships will continue as they were. It means that, whatever happens, everyone is comfortable with how the new world around them looks.

These steps are important to understand. Without that context, it would be easy to fall victim, while in our new, fragile state, to revert to previous versions of ourselves. This might involve finding ways to make the change acceptable to ourselves and others around us. We may also look for confirmation biases suggesting change is a good path to take, all while knowing deep down that these efforts would stunt our progress on the way towards our success. It will be tricky at times, but once you have mastered the art of planning your funeral each time you need to evolve, you will come back stronger and stronger each time. This allows you to leave the old view of the horizon behind, spin 180° and begin the next exciting climb.

In the next stages of our path to success, I want you to keep in mind the seven stages of grief so that your mind's eye can begin to notice them as they happen. When they appear, always put on your own gas mask first when it comes to grief. Understand your feelings and allow time to process them before attempting to help others. It will also serve you to remember that no one can be right or wrong; everyone's journey through this is different, and everyone will have their own way of managing. So be kind to yourself in these times.

When you do need to have conversations with those grieving, allow them to travel through each step without judgement and only offer guidance or assistance if requested. There are no time scales with grief, so just remember that although people might need time to adjust, the best thing you can do is support them while carrying on, not allowing anyone else's feelings to slow down your progress or journey. Just remember to be sensitive to those grieving around you.

Now we know the effects change can have on those around us. In the next chapter, we will cover how we can ensure that, while processing grief, we are changing into the best new version of ourselves.

CHAPTER 9
BURN LIST

We've just covered what can happen when we make drastic changes to ourselves on the journey to success. The good news is, now that you have prepared for this grief, an exciting step remains: the rebirth itself, shedding that proverbial skin to tackle the next climb.

You need to commit to the fact that the old you is going to need to die to make way for the new and improved version that will carry you the distance. Of course, you will be taking all the good from the old while adding the best in for the new. The best metaphor for this transformation comes from the mythical legend that is the phoenix.

The phoenix is a large, immortal bird often depicted akin to a large eagle, beautiful in its appearance and with a song that lifts the hearts of all that hear it. Yet, once every 500 to 1,000 years, the bird is engulfed in flames as it embarks on its own funeral, only to be reborn from its own ashes, renewed and transformed to an even more beautiful and elegant form. Ancient mythology points to these reincarnations after our physical deaths, but I believe we all have moments in our lives where we have the opportunity to be "reborn," taking the good from the ashes and brushing off the rest.

If we look outside myth and legend, we can also see physical representations of the same principle in the animal kingdom. Let's take snakes and lobsters as an example. For them to grow, they have to physically shed their skin, which is a slow and painful process before they emerge in a brand new layer. Other animals don't even shed skin to achieve the same effect, like the hermit crab who will adopt a new shell even if the new "shell" is a man-made object, that it will then grow into as it adapts to its new environment.

For us to begin our new climb, we, too, are going to have to go through the death of our old persona to allow our new self to rise from the ashes into the world we are looking to be successful.

Although the burn of a phoenix could be seen as destructive, when you view it in a new light, it can be quite magical. As the flames engulf the bird, it turns its entire being to ash.

As the ash settles to the floor, it becomes the fertile ground upon which a completely new phoenix can rise. The bed of ashes serves just as soil does for plants, allowing its nutrients to be soaked up to new life, leaving only the dirt behind. The new phoenix is getting all of the good with none of the bad, and that is what you are going to do in this chapter, with the help of a burn list.

A burn list is made up of two sections: "The Burn" and "The Rise." We are going consolidate all of our learnings from the book so far into what we are going to leave behind and what from the ashes we are going to take with us. The words "burn" and "rise" are chosen purposely here. I could have used "buried" and "born," I could have used "old" and "new," and I will explain why I chose the words I have shortly.

We are going to start by completing our "burn" list, and – either physically or in your mind – hold up a mirror to yourself and be as truthful as you can while creating it.

You are going to become your biggest critic. The more honest the feedback you give yourself, the more success you will have in creating a new version of yourself. This will feel uncomfortable, but the more you lean into it, the easier it becomes over time.

Write down all the limiting beliefs you have discovered by questioning the past conversations that shaped who you've become. These will be all the things that no longer serve you, things that have in the past held you back from reaching the successes you wanted in the past.

Next, note down all of the opposing traits and characteristics you have displayed that would hold you back from achieving success. This is where you really need to stare into the mirror and find all of the things you have done in the past that will not serve you now and note them down on your burn list. An example would be if you procrastinate or do not believe in yourself. These prevent you from getting started; it will be a direct blocker to who you need to become to move forwards. It can go on the list.

The last thing you need to do is revisit your stock trader's rules. These rules are going to be the things that you *must* achieve with each decision to move forwards.

I want you to look at yourself in the mirror again and note down any additional traits or characteristics that would prevent you from following your new rules.

You will now have a list that makes up all of the things you are going to be leaving behind when you complete this process. Now, it's time to focus on your "rise" list. Revisit the same moments and reflections, but, this time, note down all of the great things you realised in your discovery phase.

What did the people you spoke to actually mean and what were their true beliefs in you? If they are helpful and reinforce a part of you that is needed to reach success, write them down. From your thoughts on your version of success, take all of the great things from your list and note down what you are going to need to become in order to achieve them.

Do you need to be more forgiving to yourself?

Do you need to get started sooner?

Do you need to believe anything is possible?

Do you need to stop for breath and appreciate what is around you?

Whatever they are, put all of them down on the rise list, as this is who you are looking to become.

Now, note down all of the traits you will need to stick to your stock trader rules, adding the final steps to what should be a list that fills you with confidence and joy.

The last part I want you to add to the rise list is anything you believe would be a good addition to who you are now to help reach any of your goals. The picture you are painting is the person you have always wanted to be but believed you never could. So dream big and write it all down.

Unlike the burn list, which might have been challenging to write, the rise list should flow easily and bring an air of excitement as you are creating it. Even if you have yet to be able to envision yourself as this new person, you *want* to become them the more and more you add to the list.

Once complete, you are going to have the two sides of yourself. One is the side that you are going to be leaving behind, the old version that burns like the phoenix as it reaches the end of its life. The second is the new version, which is what will be carried forward as you are reborn like the phoenix, rising from the ashes.

So why "burn" and "rise" as opposed to "bury" and "born"?

It's not just because it fits well with the phoenix analogy. It's because of the final and fragile nature of the opposing sides. As we discovered in our last chapter, with death comes grief. It is grief that is going to try to mess with our plans as we move through the first few days, weeks and months of our rebirth.

The burn list represents you scorching these traits in your own mind and choosing to remove those parts from who you want to become. But the world around you, which is going to go through this journey at a very different pace, might see the missing parts they once knew as hidden.

We use the term "burn," as these parts are gone, never to return, removed in the most permanent way and you need to have this belief to protect your new version.

When the phoenix rises from the ashes, it isn't the same large eagle-like bird with beautiful flame-red wings. It is a smaller, more fragile infant bird, which is entering the world from the death of its predecessor, with less ability to protect itself until it grows into its adult form once more. Our rebirth will be similar. Much like the fragile infant phoenix, our new persona will be vulnerable and subject to attack from the outside world and those who are grieving for the loss of the one they once knew.

This is why we don't "bury" our list, as it could easily be dug up if the newest version of us seems too difficult to defend in the early days of its existence. It could seem like the path of least resistance. If you have a tendency to please others, it would seem like a tempting solution. Instead, we burn them so that we cannot return. But we enter our new life knowing that, in the early days, we will be vulnerable to the seven stages of grief that we and others might feel.

Now that we know what it takes to be reborn, I'm going to ask you to do what I believe is the trickiest part of not just this process, but also of growing as a successful entrepreneur or person: looking at the people you are surrounded by.

You might have read in the past that you are a reflection of the people you surround yourself with, and the reality is that's true. We tend to do two things: The first is to stretch some parts of ourselves that would not normally be present; the second is to suppress the others that do not fit the crowds we are in.

As you rise from the ashes, you are going to find your new form might no longer fit with the groups you have surrounded yourself with in the past. It's likely you will find yourself in a predicament. The people you have surrounded yourself with might have been with you for a long time, but what if they no longer fit in with who you are going to become?

The default thought I see the most and feel the most is: "It's okay, I will help them evolve as well and show them how we can do it together." I'm not going to tell you this isn't possible. Sometimes it is, but the reality is that most people resist change, especially if they have not initiated it. So, if it's you who wants them to change, you will be the one putting the effort into achieving it.

Sadly, it's only doing one thing: taking energy away from your primary goals, and ultimately, your success.

So what can be done if you find that your new form doesn't fit into the environment, and you are unable to get your environment to change? The harsh reality is, you need to move to a new environment to thrive. Let me put this into a different context to give you a less emotionally charged example.

If you take a healthy cutting from a dying plant, with a plan for it to grow back from its former glory, where would you plant it? Would you plant it in old soil with very few nutrients, in the shade with little light and water or would you choose to place it next to fresh water, rich compost, and the correct amount of sunlight? Obviously, option two is going to give it the best chance at survival. So why would we do any differently with the newest version of ourselves?

You might be thinking that this is easy in principle, but the reality of removing those close to you who will no longer give you the nutrient-rich environment to grow is tough. I won't lie to you. *It is not easy.* The good news is, unlike your burn list, you don't need to permanently remove these people from your world.

The reason is that it is not realistic and, by doing so, you will likely expend as much energy in trying to remove them as you would trying to change them. But what can you do to get the best results without offending or causing issues with those you already have around you?

The answer is to allocate more time to finding and surrounding yourself with the right kind of people. The more time put into this, the less time you will spend with those who hold you back, and more with those who help you grow.

If the people you used to surround yourself with follow you into the new circles, that is fantastic as you didn't use your energy to do it. They saw you thriving in a better situation and chose to be reborn themselves.

For those who don't want to change but want to remain the same, they will continue as they are. You will slowly and naturally spend less time with them as they travel through the grief process and focus their energy on others who match their goals and aspirations.

You might be wondering how you are going to find the new people to surround yourself with; everyone's circles' needs will look different.

The thing to focus on is ensuring that your new friends and acquaintances embody what you are trying to become. They should be at least a few steps ahead of you in becoming that type of person.

If you aim for people who are in your position and aspiring to grow, you might meet some awesome people but might not gain a great deal (though one awesome exception is when you find someone to share the journey with). If you aim for people who are where you want to be in a few months' or years' time, the worst that can happen is that you end up the same as them.

The best-case scenario is you end up surpassing them. It is either that or they grow at the same rate you do and you are continually moving forwards.

As you begin to spend more time with these people, those whom you used to allocate the majority of your time will have had time to grieve, and those who are still important to you and reciprocate that feeling will remain in your lives to still share moments and memories, allowing you to grow into your new skin without being held back.

CHAPTER 10
EVOLUTION, A STEP-BY-STEP GUIDE

Take a deep breath, hold it, then exhale deeply.

Just like that breath, the weight of allowing yourself to be recreated might be a heavy task. But once you have, the release of the change, much like the air rushing from your lungs, feels like a weight being lifted.

As we move into this chapter, with the hard work you've put in in all the chapters so far, it's now time to have an air of excitement about what's to come. The mountain peak of success is high above you, but you can see it clearly in all of its glory. The excitement of climbing can now be your driving force each day.

As we are about to tread into uncharted territory, there will likely be some nerves that come with the "new you" and the journey you are about to travel. And even though we have set ourselves up for success, that mountain peak might still seem a long way off. Unlike the strong and capable phoenix that carried you here, you might be fragile and fresh, but your rebirth and new self have the tools needed to take your first steps and come with an abundance of new energy and belief that will propel you forward.

With that end goal now clear, this chapter is here to help you understand everything there is to know about the climb you'll need to make to the peak of that mountain. That mountain is the destination you plugged into our Personal Success Sat-Nav. This chapter will also describe what you'll need at each stage to make the climb as simple as possible.

New journeys come with new challenges, and the likelihood is the skills needed to traverse these advanced rock faces and caverns will be a new playground for you to explore. Just as with any journey and task, the more time you can spend in advance planning and honing your skills, the less time and pain comes during the journey. There is a famous story that illustrates this well, which is a story of two lumberjacks working side by side.

Each lumberjack is tasked with chopping the same style and thickness of wood; each has the same hours each day with which to complete this task. Lumberjack 1 starts work every day at 9am sharp. He is on time and ready to go, and he continues at a strong and steady pace for the full day until 5pm without taking a break. His consistency brings him good results, with his eight full hours of chopping time producing 1,000 perfectly chopped logs at the end of each day.

Lumberjack 2 also starts his day at 9am sharp, so he is also on time and ready to go. He also works at the same pace and consistency as Lumberjack 1. The only difference is that each day, he leaves the site at 12pm for a one-hour lunch break, returning at 1pm sharp to continue his work in the same manner from where he left it. At the end of each day, he has completed seven hours of chopping wood, and his labour consistently produces 1,200 perfectly chopped logs.

This goes on for a number of weeks, with the same results repeating each day. Lumberjack 1 begins to get frustrated, trying everything to produce the same number of logs as his coworker. He tries chopping the wood faster than he had previously but finds that, by 3pm each day, he is too tired and spends the remaining two hours finishing his work at a slower pace, still only producing 1,000 logs. He tries chopping multiple logs at the same time but finds he spends more time fixing errors at the end of each day, which brings his total down to only 900 perfect logs.

Finally, enough is enough. Before the lumberjacks embark on their next day's work, the first asks, "How is it you consistently work one hour less than me, but produce 20% more at the end of each day? Where do you go at 12pm and what do you do with that hour?"

The second lumberjack laughs and replies, "I go home and do the same thing I do each morning before we start the day. I go to my workshop and spend the hour sharpening my axe. Each time I swing my axe, the sharpened blade makes each cut cleaner and more effective – meaning I do less work, for more results."

The moral of this story? Sharpened honed tools wielded by a skilled person will get any job done more efficiently than unprepared tools in the same hands. Abraham Lincoln was famously quoted as saying, "Give me six hours to chop down a tree and I will spend the first four sharpening the axe." For the same reasons as in the story, he knew that spending the time ahead of the task learning and sharpening his tools would save the effort needed during the work. Still, there are going to be very few readers of this book who are going to use an axe day to day to get their jobs done. So how do we translate this into your own blueprint to success, when the road ahead is uncharted?

The way we are going to accomplish this is by chunking the journey up into phases. Before you begin each phase, you need to look at what's ahead and find ways to rapidly evolve yourself and your skill set before you take your first steps into the task at hand (i.e. sharpening our metaphorical axe). So, if you are going to evolve, we first need to understand what that means.

Evolution in its traditional sense simply means the slow and gradual development of something to suit its environment. We see it most used in the concept of human and natural organisms development. It's believed that all species had to physically change and adapt to survive and thrive in whatever environment they found themselves in. They did not only have to change to survive but they also had no real idea of what they needed to become until they had struggled along for hundreds of years as evolution ran its course.

One of the most documented examples of evolution is the peppered moth, which, pre-1800s, had light, mottled wings, displaying both light and dark patterns, with only a small number being black entirely. Yet, after the Industrial Revolution, the most common version of a peppered moth was darker, with the lighter versions becoming rarer due to the increased pollution. The moths needed to be able to blend into the now more soot-covered surfaces, with scientists discovering that this was due to mutated genes within the moth's body, forced by the need to survive in its newfound environment.

It's not just colours that change either. Animals have also been documented to have adapted preexisting limbs to be used for other activities or be used in new environments, like webbing between the toes for animals that live or hunt in water.

The good news is that you don't need to endure pain to evolve; you won't need webbed feet or a new colour. It's your traits and skill set that need to evolve. So, unlike the peppered moth, which adapted as it met its challenges and as time went on, we can pre-plan each phase to preempt what skills and tools we will need to make each phase of the climb as simple as possible.

That is exactly what we are going to do: Map out the path before you climb it and understand what is going to be needed from us for that to happen. We are going to create our step-by-step guide to the evolutions you will need for each part of the journey, with the hope that if you understand and plan for what's to come, the journey will be a whole lot easier to manage. This will apply to large journeys that span a number of years, or mini-journeys that take only a few weeks or months. Regardless, the process is going to be treated exactly the same. The end result will always be to create a plan that you can manoeuvre through as you aim for the next heights of success by following the 3-Step Evolution Plan below.

Your 3-Step Evolution Plan

Step 1: Evolution Space

The first thing you need to do is write down your starting point and the date (where you are today) as well as your Personal Success Sat-Nav destination as the endpoint, including the date you intend to arrive. The bit that is in between these two points is your evolution space, and this is where you are going to focus your time and effort before you take the first steps. Whether this will take months or years, it is absolutely fine. You just need to ensure you've highlighted the time available to complete the evolution.

Step 2: Chunking

We are going to use the chunking method to break the journey down. Chunking refers to the process of splitting up one large task into smaller, more manageable ones. For example, instead of trying to read 100 pages of this book all at once, you could chunk the task to make it more manageable. This might be equally divvying up the reading over the course of five days and choosing to read 20 pages per day.

Everyone's evolution journey will have a different number of chunks that it can be split into, but don't worry. I am going to teach you a method in this step that will allow you to chunk it up into a manageable amount that fits your journey's needs. To do this, you first need to add some more context of success to your start- and endpoints, which needs to be the best possible measure of your success.

For many, this will be a financial target. For others, this might be a measure of health or a number of other things. Whatever the metric is, this will be our main focal point of success and will be treated as our main KPI (key performance indicator). For this example, we will use a financial marker. The starting point will be £0 and the finish line will be £100,000. Once added, the next step is to add the halfway point between the two, which in this example would be £50,000 in revenue. If your goal is a fitness goal like weight, this will be the halfway measure between your existing and goal weights.

You now have our first two chunks, the beginning half and final half of your evolution journey. With the same method, you are now going to split each half of the journey again to give yourself four chunks to work with. So, for our example, you now have increments of £25k of revenue per chunk making them £0-£25k, £25k-£50k, £50k-£75k and the final chunk of £75k to our £100k goal. This is the first point where you will be able to evaluate the skills and tasks needed to complete each chunk, and I want you to test yours like I am about to in the below example.

Let's assume you are trying to get from a standing start of zero to our first £25,000 in revenue, the first chunk. For this example, let's imagine that you are at the start of your journey from a nine-to-five employee to a startup business owner. The first thing is to look at the target to complete this chunk. Is it something that seems to be achievable with a little effort, or does it feel as far away as the end peak that you are trying to climb? If you feel overwhelmed by it, go back to splitting the chunks down, going from quarters to 1/8th. Then re-evaluate it. If that doesn't seem achievable, go one step further and break it down to tenths. You can go even further, splitting equally before continuing. At this point, it would look like £0-£10k-£20k, etc. Each chunk should be manageable when you stretch yourself and your ability.

Step 3: Sharpening the Axe

When you are happy with your chunking, it's time to start planning your evolution *ahead* of each chunk. This is the equivalent of sharpening the axe before each shift of chopping wood. The sharper the axe, the easier the chop. This is called the WWH method: where, what and how, and there are three parts to this exercise which need to be applied to one chunk at a time. Only move to the next one once you have physically reached the milestone at the end of the chunk in your journey.

In order to plan the "how" and "what", you will need to sharpen your axe for each chunk. You will need to run each of them through the following three phases of questions.

Phase 1: Where are you now?

- What are the skills that have got you to where you are today?

- With the skills you have, how close will you be able to get to your next target?

Phase one is a good point to reflect on the skills you have relied on heavily to reach your current ceiling and understand to what extent they will support you to reach your next. These skills will still likely make up 70% of what you will need to achieve the next chunk, unless you are pivoting in a new direction. If you are pivoting direction, you will be looking at your existing skills to see which are transferable to your new destination.

Phase 2: What is missing?

- Looking at the destination, what challenges will you have to overcome?

- What skills do you need to close the gap between the point with your existing skill set and where you need to be in the end?

- What other skills could make the climb not just achievable, but easier?

Phase two is where you have to apply as much humble honesty as possible. Hold the mirror up to yourself to search for the gaps and imperfections in our existing arsenal of skills and evaluate them to see what other skills might make our lives easier moving forwards.

Phase 3: How can I fix it?

- Where can you go to learn the skills needed?

- Who already has these skills that you could speak to?

The final phase is where you change from reflection to research, and you are able to explore the avenues you need to tread, to upskill yourself or surround yourself with those who can plug the gap. The people you find could be a contractor, an employee, or a mentor who will educate you.

Once you have completed all three phases for the chunk you are focusing on, you will have a robust understanding of not just what you have available to you, but where and how you are going to plug the existing gaps.

So before even taking our first steps to success, you now have:

- A detailed understanding of the terrain ahead and what it will take to conquer them.

- What you are going to upskill in and what existing skills you are going to lean on.

- The people you need around you to support you in your journey.

You now have a step-by-step guide to your evolution that you can begin to take action on immediately, rather than the traditional method of "thinking on our feet" when you hit the issues head-on. By understanding the areas you will get stuck at and preparing for them in advance, you are given the opportunity to not only move through the tough spots quickly but also make the journey feel a hell of a lot easier. This allows you to keep balance in your Health, Wealth and Happiness Triangle, rather than need to swing the pendulum at the problem, which in turn pulls away from other areas of your life.

There will, of course, be bumps in the road to success. No matter how much we plan ahead, we can never see all of them ahead of time. But by filling in the largest gaps, you make the smaller, unseen ones more manageable, as you have freed up your time by not having to think on your feet with the problems we have already solved.

We will go through this step-by-step evolution guide for each chunk, focusing on and completing them before moving on to the next so as to not overwhelm with the change needed. Once you nail the WWH method, it will take you no time at all to complete each chunk. Eventually, this is something you will do intuitively even outside of your roadmap to success. I often find myself working this method in my head for everyday tasks like planning a weekend away with my wife and children. The result is that we always have a great time with all the little gaps plugged in so we can focus on being together.

It is also a great tool to reflect and give gratitude for everything that has been accomplished so far. As entrepreneurs, business owners and those who want more success from everyday life, our hunger for success often means we often spend our time looking and moving forwards, rather than stopping to appreciate the view of the climb we have just surmounted. The "what" allows us that breathing space to appreciate the skills we have developed and where they have led us before we get ready for the next charge forward.

Focusing chunk by chunk makes the overall journey feel somehow easy. We know we will get to the end goal, so we can take our focus and wander away from the finish line. If we just apply our time to the pre-evolution plan and make the climb as easy as possible, success at the end of the journey is practically guaranteed. All we have to do is make sure we have the right tools to keep putting one foot in front of the other.

For this exercise, you can head over to our free resources area where you can download our free evolution planner via this link:

www.lifestyle-entrepreneur.co.uk/stp.

CHAPTER 11
MENTOR ME

The question I'm asked more than any other, and the one I hear asked of other entrepreneurs at events and seminars, is "How do you find your mentors?" I myself used to ask the very same question when given the opportunity to speak to someone I admired or looked up to. How was it they managed to not only find but enrol these amazing people as mentors, to teach them all the wonderful things that had led to their success?

I can also see why people would want to know the secret behind this: to peer behind the curtain and find out how you connect with these high net worth individuals, or the intellects that hold all of the answers to the problems you have yet to encounter on your journey. Who in their right mind wouldn't want to know the secret to finding them if it gave you a shortcut to success?

Well, the good news is, by the end of this chapter you will know exactly where to look for these mentors and how to find them.

Before we get to that, it's important to understand what leads people to ask this question in the first place. Why do you actually need a mentor?

Mentors are the equivalent of a shortcut on a long journey, the cheat code on your favourite video game or the tips and hints you might be given in a murder mystery. Mentors are people who, when chosen correctly, can open doors for you, accelerate your journey and steer you away from the wrong paths.

Mentors are the number one resource or tool that you cannot create for yourself, who will aid in accelerating your journey to success, and, at times, allow you to surpass what you believed was possible.

So let's look at what a mentor actually is, and by virtue what it isn't, starting with the definition.

Mentor, n. An experienced and trusted adviser.

A mentor is not to be mistaken for a coach, who is a person who teaches and trains an individual or team while supporting the decision-making process.

Mentors offer guidance to the path we are looking to tread, usually speaking from the experience of having walked it before. In the traditional meaning, a mentor is a navigator, not a task manager; they are a sounding board, not a problem solver. Think of them as the guide whose sole purpose is to find and use your internal greatness, mixed with their experience, to accelerate your external results.

So, we know mentors have been in our shoes, have already walked the path we are looking to pursue, and have vast experience in either our field or in general. Now how about the type of person they are? Do they need to share your exact vision and goals? Do they need to be vastly wealthy? Do they need to be a public figure?

The reality and answer to all of these questions is no, they don't. A mentor can be rich or poor, at the peak of health or not. They don't even have to be known for what they do (which I think is the first misconception of mentors). None of these things are a requirement.

What I am not saying here is that they won't have these things; in reality, when chasing success, the people above you *are* likely to have these things. These are just not the first criteria we look for.

A mentor can be *anyone* you can learn from. They just have to be ahead of you in the journey you are looking to take, and you have to respect and admire the way they approached their existing and onward progression, which will be reciprocated by them taking an interest in yours.

Where might you already have one of these possible mentors? Who is further down the path, has a genuine interest in your success, and is someone you look up to?

If you are lucky enough to have been bought into a loving home, then your parents would have played this role. Sacrificing years of their lives, dedicating them to your ongoing development and overall success as a human, parents are usually the biggest cheerleaders, guides and mentors of their children. They work tirelessly to open up opportunities through guidance and care, and if you had not realised it until reading this chapter, you already had/have one or two mentors in your life.

If you look further afield into your community, you might also find some more there too. They might be siblings, they could be extended family or even those in your close friend network that you admire or aspire to be like. Even if they are not in your field of expertise or want to take the same path as you, you can sometimes find mentors who have one characteristic you admire and want to emulate. If you don't have these yet, start looking harder at the people you surround yourself with and tune in to the things you admire about these people.

Ask questions and learn all the skills you can from them, as these mentors are going to be already personally invested in your success.

This in part is how I found my first mentor Angie. To this day, she is still one of the main reasons I am successful. She was able to unlock a part of me that believed I *could* be successful, all because *she* saw that part of me, and knew I just needed to be re-introduced to it.

I was in my early twenties. At the time, I was working with my brother to build his business in the property industry. I was an *expert* in delivering as an employee, going over and above in everything I did. But at this stage, I would never have dreamed of owning a business myself.

My family could see promise in me, the more we worked together, the more they saw the value I could deliver. But my lack of belief was my main limiting factor in leading a team, so they sought the advice of my

Auntie Angie, who was an expert and published author in this field.

Angie agreed to coach me and a group of other people who were at a similar level to me, also family and friends. We would meet and cover high-level leadership styles, profiling and strategies that could help with building and leading a team.

The sessions were gold; I took a ton of useful information away from them. Still, it was Angie who took the time to evaluate the group and identify outside of the strategies and lessons, what it was about us as individuals that held us back. It was then we began working in a more one-on-one setting, with Angie moving from coach to mentor.

I still believe it is what I learnt about myself in those one-on-one sessions that has allowed me to create a successful path, and eventually, to write this book. Angie unlocked parts of my mind and belief system that, if left undiscovered, would have remained with a tight grip, holding me back from what I was really capable of. I owe a lot to Angie, and I am truly grateful to her.

You might be thinking, "Well, it's alright for you. You had an exceptional mentor in your immediate family, I don't have that." That is not something I will not argue with; there was an element of luck in me getting that dedicated focus from someone so valuable. But it is *how* Angie worked with me that might change your perspective and help you realise these people exist in your network too.

In the sessions with Angie, she didn't use complex strategies to identify my deepest flaws. She didn't get me to do tests or solve problems that would highlight them. She didn't use complex technology or AI to analyse the things I said to her. She only had one tool that was always present, which was a hot cup of tea paired with a couple of chocolate biscuits.

Each session I would arrive at Angie's home, she would welcome me in and we would sit in her living room having a catch-up. We would talk first about the general day-to-day of our lives, how things are going and the things that had happened since we last saw each other. Then we would talk about work, covering the things that were going well and the things that were not going so well.

When we covered each topic that required improvement, we would explore what it was about that subject that I felt was holding me back – whether it was a real barrier or one I was creating for myself.

Depending on which it was, we would find either a practical solution to the real problems or a clever way to get around the ones I was making for myself. It was really that simple (well, at least Angie made it seem that way). Angie was facilitating the conversations that allowed me to explore what was blocking my path, and then together we were finding ways that worked for me to remove them altogether.

Angie was always fantastic at this. Every session, I left with a new little trick or tactic to unlock another part of my forward journey. Those parts soon added up to more confidence, fewer barriers, and more belief. It really was that simple, and if you have someone in your life who is willing to take a genuine interest in you, willing to challenge you on the validity of the things that hold you back and can make a cracking cup of tea, the likelihood is they could be a mentor to you.

To give you an understanding of how simple these solutions were, I will share one of the biggest takeaways I took from my time with Angie so that if it is applicable to you, you can use it. And if it isn't, you can at least understand how these small things can make a huge difference.

The Joker

During most of our sessions, my limiting beliefs would come up in conversation. And this is something that we'd often tune into. In this particular session, I was talking to Angie about a presentation I had to do in our company's boardroom. It was to be in front of the entire organisation, which did not consist only of my peers.

As it was a family business, I would have to present to them too, and at the time this terrified me. Angie looked over the draft presentation and sung its praises, believing it would likely be well received by all, so we dug into why it made me feel this way. We discovered it was because the person I saw standing at the front of the room, attempting to speak, was a much younger, less successful version of myself.

At this point in my career, I was in a good position, running a team and making a big difference in the business. Yet the person on the stage in my mind was the kid who left school with very little grades, no confidence and was three or four doughnuts past the overweight category. This version of me did exist, but it should have been left in the past.

Unfortunately, day to day, this was still how I perceived myself. In my mind, this person had no place being in the position I was in. I felt like an imposter.

So rather than just reassure me that I was no longer that person, Angie set me a simple task: Turn up to our next session with an object that represents that version of me. The only criterion is that it was small enough to fit in the palm of my hand.

I did as I was asked, and after some time and deep thought and soul searching, the best I could come up with was that the old version of me was a bit of a joker. Great at making people smile and being a clown, but when it came to it, that's all I felt I was. So I bought a Lego keyring of the Joker from Batman, and took it along to my next session.

The session happened as normal, Angie and I caught up about the day-to-day things that had been happening, and she looked through my finalised presentation, correcting all of the spelling mistakes and grammar (which came embarrassingly in large volumes). It was only at the end of the session that Angie asked me to produce my homework. I handed over my Joker keyring and explained how I believed it embodied the version of me that always presented itself when I tried to speak publicly or when I was in a position that required me to show authority. Angie looked it over while she listened.

When I was done with my explanation, she simply acknowledged that the Joker keyring was a previous version of me. After placing it down on the table, she finished the remaining dregs of the tea in her cup, inverted it, and then placed it on top of the keyring so that it couldn't be seen. The idea was that this version of me still existed, but it was now unable to get to me because it served no value or purpose in today's reality. She explained that the presentation was fantastic (especially now that it had no spelling mistakes) and its message was clear. The only thing that had to happen was that the version of me who sat in front of her, not under the teacup, had to read it out.

So I did just that. With confidence and without faltering, I ran through the entire presentation, and when I got to the end, I realised the only thing that was preventing me from doing this before this session was me – an old version of me that no longer mattered. The Joker under the cup was a physical reminder for me of how far I had come, and that I was no longer the same man I once was.

I used this little "trick" for many years, carrying the Joker around with me until I no longer needed him at all and was able to take him off my keyring and leave him behind. There were more keyrings that followed, which helped me unlock other limiting beliefs and served as reminders as I travelled my path. And they all came from simple facilitated conversations with Angie. These all had the purpose of identifying and alleviating blockers to my self-belief. Even to this day, I now buy myself a keyring that embodies where I am heading or what is holding me back as a daily reminder to push me forwards.

This was my very first taste of a personal mentor, and you may or may not have had this yourself. The key now will be to tune into who around you could help unlock your beliefs, and help support your journey. In our communities and programs, we spend a large amount of time on mindset and limiting beliefs, because I know from personal experience it is one of the easiest and quickest accelerators of any success journey. And it all starts from within.

Mentors don't just need to be friends and family either, there's also the opportunity to pay for mentorship. I have personally invested tens of thousands of pounds over the years in my ongoing education, both personally and professionally. I would love to share all of the nuggets I have learnt, but they alone would fill another book, let alone the rest of this chapter.

Instead, I will share with you the four musts when searching for a paid mentor, regardless of whether you are spending £10 or £100,000 on mentorship. Because without them, you will not be getting your money's worth.

The 4 Musts of a Mentor

1. Ultimate Alignment

When you are approaching paid mentorship, you need to make sure that the mentors' personal or company values align with your own. This is an important step to make sure you can confidently implement the lessons in your own life. If they don't align, the likely result is you will get teachings that will drag you off your path rather than speed up your success. There will always be multiple options when you look to learn from someone. For example, you could be spending your time reading someone else's book on how to be successful. I'm hoping you chose mine because in some way you connected with me on a personal level or one of my business's values matched your own.

2. Curiosity Killed the Cat, Not Us!

The second thing you need to be prepared for is to be curious. The famous saying "curiosity killed the cat" was not designed for the hungry entrepreneur, yet we need to be more curious than ever in day-to-day life, and that doesn't stop when it comes to mentorship. Mentors and teachers choose to share their wisdom with the world because they have a desire to help and support people. They will often come prepared to teach you about something you've signed up for, but understand this is likely 10% of their real-life experiences. And there is so much you can learn from just asking good questions. Questions that get them to think deeply and respond with value that would not normally be shared, like "What was the one thing that sits in the back of your mind when you consider why you became an entrepreneur?" or "What started as your most important reason for starting a business, and what is it now?" Questions like these will spark conversations and responses that will teach you so much about their journey and how they might be able to help you. Mentors want to share, so create sparks that give them reasons to.

3. There Is No Hero in This Movie

The phrase "Never meet your heroes" is more relevant here than anywhere else. There are very few people who walk this earth who in reality would match up to the pedestal you put them on. We are all human, we all have flaws. The likelihood is that, if you focus enough and learn from the right people, you should be able to exceed their accomplishments. If you view mentors as regular people you can learn from, you will glean so much more from them and will make nearly any mentor you want accessible to you.

4. Mentorship Is a Two-way Street

You should never underestimate the value *you* also offer a mentor, and I am not talking about what you can offer financially. Although you have not monetised your experiences, they have real value to the mentor you are sharing them with and there are two examples that spring to mind for this.

The first is a personal one, which comes from when I was working in our family business that was owned and operated by my brother. I had moved with my then fiancée to Nottingham to work in the business to support its growth. During the time I worked for my brother, I got married and we welcomed our first son into the world.

My brother and I were both on different trajectories. He was putting his time and focus purely into his business, spending every waking minute of the day strategising how to grow and expand his empire to secure his financial freedom. This was infectious to me, as it is something I also aspired for.

Above this, my focus was on having and raising a family, which saw us both on similar paths but with different amounts of energy in each. For him, it was 90% business with 10% personal; for me, it was more like 50-50, with my work hours being fully committed to learning and growth, but my time at home was dedicated to being a husband and father.

I looked up to my brother, Dan. I loved his freedom, his lifestyle, what he had created and his aspirations to constantly take it to the next level. There were times I was jealous of his success, even though I was always a supporter of it. I would be lying if I said I didn't want a piece of it for myself, which is why the next part of the story was the biggest shock to me.

It was a weekend and Dan and I had headed to a gym together. Afterwards, we decided to have a dip in the pool. As always, Dan took a notepad and pen to stash at the side of the pool so that when our conversations about work struck some gold, he could jot them down to come back to them later. Given Dan's hunger for business back then, most of our conversations would be focused on the company or business in general (which we both enjoyed).

It came up in the conversation about how similar we were and the paths we had taken. To my surprise, on this occasion, Dan turned to me and said something I had not expected. He told me that he aspired to be like me someday.

This took me aback. How could he want to be like me? He had the company, the fast car, the money – what could I possibly have that he couldn't get for himself?

For him, it was my ability to put my family ahead of myself and my ambition. It is something he was envious of at that point in his life, as the ability to do it evaded him. Our paths were so different, but fundamentally we were not.

We were raised in the same home, but his focus was on financial success; whereas mine at that time was on the success of starting and raising a family. We both stood from different perspectives and had as much to learn from each other as we had to offer. Similarly, when you approach mentorship, it will serve you well to remember that both parties bring equal value and likely underestimate its worth.

The second example I can give comes from an online video in which a YouTube influencer is interviewing the legend that is Elon Musk. They are walking through the grounds of SpaceX and Elon is explaining how you don't require a cold gas thruster system when you have hot gas. Then, the influencer asks the simple question, "That's just on the booster, right?"

Elon pauses and realises they have missed a huge opportunity. This is because their focus was too close to the project, and they should consider this for the ship itself. The interviewer essentially facilitated the conversation to make Elon realise there was a missed opportunity that could save and make him millions of pounds – all because he was curious and asked good questions.

The advice I would give you from these two examples is to be interested and to be interesting. Know the value you bring and find ways that can make it interesting to other people. Figure out in the least number of words how you can describe who you are, what you stand for and what you do, and then be five times more interested in hearing about other people over your own. This will open doors that you didn't know you were looking for. Just practising this little gem in your day-to-day life will open so many opportunities. If it doesn't, at least you have broadened your network and hopefully shared some value.

Meeting mentors in your existing networks or via networking is not the only way you can find them. There is one way that requires very little effort and can be done from anywhere in the world. And the best thing is, you don't have to pay anything – you don't even have to meet them!

We live in a world where we are fortunate enough to see behind the scenes of some of the most successful celebrities, visionaries and business moguls. And as long as you choose the right ones that fit your values, there will be hours and hours of content available online that can serve your need for a mentor.

You won't be able to ask direct questions to these people, but you will be able to watch interviews and clips where they explain their methods and thinking. The more you watch, the more commonalities in the way they operate will be made clear, which, once you pick up on, might serve your thinking as you approach your journey. You have access to *millions* of mentors in the little device in your pocket.

If you spent that time watching and learning from the people who are ahead of you, rather than doom-scroll on social media, you might be able to replicate some of their success just by learning how they go about their business and what they share in their online content.

So, to answer the most common question, "Where do you find your mentors?" The answer is *everywhere*.

The more you open your mind to the value you can get from others, the more opportunities will come to you to land yourself a stellar mentor.

CHAPTER 12
THE LAST PIECE OF THE JIGSAW PUZZLE

This is our penultimate chapter, and I'd first like to thank and congratulate you for reading this far. I have written this book as a practical guide to assist you in finding your own success, without the need for copying the routines of others who have become successful. I once tried to follow Mark Wahlburg's daily workout routine. If you have ever thought about trying it, I must warn you, it is not for the faint-hearted! I lasted one day… just one day of trying to be successful by wearing someone else's shoes, before I realised it didn't matter if I'd lasted a day or even a year. Though I would undoubtedly see *some* success, for me, this would be like pushing treacle uphill. It was so out of flow for me that it would not have been enjoyable at all, and I would be sacrificing my happiness for success.

This is one of the things that led me to create the blueprints and methods you have learned in this book so far. When implemented and practised, they will allow you to carve out your own path to success by leaning on the things you are *great* at, rather than trying to mimic the actions of those who are already successful. It might not be as sexy as posting on Instagram about your 5am monk routine or feel as liberating as finding enlightenment through meditation. But it will get the job done while keeping you grounded, balanced and constantly accountable to yourself and those you choose to spend your life with – all while unlocking levels of success that others only dream about.

This chapter is slightly different from the others, as I am not going to give you a method or a task to complete as we approach your steps to success. Instead, I am going to teach you something a lot more valuable, which I believe if I were to leave it out of this book, would lay waste to your existing hard work regardless of the health, wealth and happiness you obtain from what you have already applied. This lesson will allow your overall success to feel complete. Even though you might not feel its effects at the beginning, you will as you chase your next level and embrace all of the excitement that comes with the journey. The only thing that is more important than this one thing is sticky toffee pudding! (But we will talk about that later.) It is the reason humans are currently at the top of the food chain. And it is one of the reasons – other than your sex and status drive – that you are reading this book.

It all starts with the hunger for more.

We all want more in our lives: more time, more money, more love, more sex, more jewellery, more admiration, more quiet, more noise, more, more, more, more, more. As humans, it is pre-programmed into us to strive for more. Some of us have a larger hunger for it than others, with some being content with the basics and others wanting to conquer the world. Whichever category you fit into, this will be relevant. But if you are anything like me and you have an insatiable appetite for growth, this will be game-changing. What this chapter is going to focus on is *why* we always want more, regardless of how much we obtain. Without a shift in perspective, you will always be searching for the missing piece of the jigsaw.

Imagine putting together a 10,000-piece jigsaw puzzle, only to be missing the very last piece you need to complete the magnificent picture you have constructed over thousands of hours. This can be the reality for all who set out to be successful. You realise that when you arrive at success, you feel like a piece is missing. It can consume you in a search that will never bear fruit and, at its worst, send you down a path you never intended, trying to fill that newly discovered void. This chapter will help you avoid this by giving you an understanding of what that missing piece really is.

As I write this chapter, it's 4:29am and my family are all soundly asleep. Yet I am wide awake and have been since 3am, with a mind full of ideas and business growth plans buzzing around like flies, fighting for my imagination's attention. Entrepreneurship has given me a lot of gifts over the years, but one of the curses is the inability to "switch off" my brain. When it decides it's time to play business, there isn't much I can do to convince it otherwise! This is something that I could take as a negative. Instead, I have learnt over the years it's simply how I'm built and something I now embrace to its fullest extent. I even celebrate the idea that I don't operate like a "normal person," enjoying these moments when they happen.

So as I sit in my living room with just a laptop screen illuminating the space, and with my fingers tapping away on the keyboard being the only noise that can be heard, you might ask why, of all the things I could do with my time, have I chosen to write this chapter? It's because, although you might not experience the same 3am awakenings as I do on my journey, the thing we will all have in common is that irrefutable human desire to search and grow.

Let me take you back to the starting years of one of my businesses and the moments that immediately preceded my first levels of success. The business in question is one of our e-commerce businesses that leverages the Amazon FBA platform as the main source of revenue. It still remains as one of the majority contributors to my overall business cash flow.

This business's life started in my garden shed during lockdown as a project to see what was possible using the Amazon FBA business model. It was also a way for me and my long-term friend Kunal Dattani to reconnect on a business level and explore working together. The model is simple enough: Create a unique product within an existing marketplace and take a percentage of the sales that are currently going to competitors in the platform. The better you are at creating and branding unique products, the better results you get.

Kunal and I both had ambitions to work together in the long term on numerous projects, and we were using this as an opportunity to explore how well we connected on values, work ethic and overall support for each other. We started speaking daily between our other commitments, and it only took a few calls before we identified an opportunity on the Amazon platform that we could use to launch our own branded product. However, given it was lockdown, it wasn't going to be easy with most of the world closed for business. We spent a few more weeks of research, catch-up calls, and negotiating with suppliers to convince them to work with us as a new customer. We managed to get stock to us while navigating the complex ever-changing rules and regulations during lockdown, and we were starting to see potential. Around eight weeks had passed and we had brought our ideas to life. Before we knew it, our first batch of inventory and the materials to package it were delivered to my door, ready to be prepared for sale. (It's still in my garden shed now!)

I got the family involved in the process and my son was helping me fill bags and label products, loving every minute. Meanwhile my wife had nervous trepidations about what I was getting myself into and how this could even be possible in a world where we couldn't leave the house. Finally, the goods were ready, and we booked a UPS driver to collect the stock and send it to Amazon.

Then we waited…and waited…and waited for what felt like weeks for the stock to make it onto Amazon's shelves and become available to the general public. This in itself felt like a success that should be celebrated but the real shock came a few days later, when the stock actually started to sell!

So, I'm in my shed with a dodgy lockdown haircut, on a Zoom call with Kunal, dancing and celebrating that we had sold four units of stock! This to me was INSANE, that we could take an idea that we found online, and with a few weeks of work, could turn that idea into a viable cash flowing business model. At this point, we had made £39.96 in revenue which would result in around £13.18 in profit – not much to write home about. The reason I was dancing like a dad at a wedding was because we had done something that seemed impossible, yet made it a reality.

That product in its first year of existence would go on to make £92,000 in revenue, yielding £32,000 in profits. It is still a product we sell to this day. What's even more incredible is that, to get it started and listed on Amazon, we only invested £500 collectively, both stumping up £250 of our hard earned cash to get the business off the ground. This is why this is still the business we put a lot of our focus into day to day, as the ability to generate cash flow is off the charts.

With this early success under our belts, Kunal and I were both in. We were making good money, we were working well together, and the opportunity to do something was in front of us. So, as soon as we were physically able and allowed to by the UK government, we locked ourselves in a well-ventilated room, planned out the next year of business together, and put forward the target revenues and profits we wanted to hit. Fast forward to February 2022, a few days before my birthday. I had just picked up the keys to a new unit and office which was going to house our business expansion. SUCCESS!

This was the first major milestone and success I had felt in this business and it was *amazing.* The office itself was certainly far from amazing, though: it was in a local industrial estate, measured 550 square feet and had zero outside windows. The only window it had was out into an internal corridor which led to the other businesses on my floor. Nevertheless, to me, it was perfect. I quickly filled the office with the basic furniture I needed, painted it to look the best it could and added some LED lighting (for no other reason than I thought it was cool – and still do!). The business was now turning over around £20,000 a month and was well established in its industry, with heavy growth plans already in place to raise that monthly amount to £100,000 in the next 12 months. I was making friends with other businesses in the unit and had begun to train in the private gym downstairs from my office. I was also walking to and from work each day, so the lockdown weight was already diminished, and I was overall in good shape.

"The Cave" quickly became the office's nickname, and my close friends who could now work from home often came to the office for the day to work alongside me. (It might also have had something to do with the pole dancing studio that was situated next door, which happened to be the view we had from our only internal window.) Either way, life was good! I was healthy, generating wealth and happy…

…but something was missing.

It was around April when I first noticed it. The business had already gone through another phase of growth, and although everything was still on the up, I found myself in a slump. The business is in a position where we nailed the processes and it was running like clockwork. Although we were putting a fair amount of time into it, all was in flow and felt easy. Yet, I found myself procrastinating from time to time, searching YouTube or getting lost in an Instagram reel hole, with an hour passing before I would look up and realise that I was not being productive. I was in the biggest opportunity of my life at the time, yet I was wasting it with distractions and shiny objects, rather than knuckling down and getting shit done.

I think of myself as a reasonably intelligent guy, so how could I be letting this happen? It had taken me a lot of effort to climb the first mountain. But I was neither enjoying the view nor sizing up the next summit. I was just kicking my feet in the mud which, if left unchecked, would inevitably slide me back down the cliff face that I had just scaled. Have you ever been in that situation, where everything is going well, you have everything lined up and singing in harmony and even looking like it's going to get better. Then you get either complacent or start to find faults around you?

You might have set yourself a goal or a task. When you arrive at the destination through hard work and focus, you would expect that to motivate you onwards and upwards. Instead, it just doesn't happen. This is where I found myself. I was happy with how much ground I had covered in such a short space of time. Everyone around me was congratulating me and telling me how awesome it was to see, yet I was just a little bit… meh. There are two reasons I felt this, and they might be similar to your own experiences.

The first is the anticlimax of arriving at success. We all dream of the ticker tape parade and the admiration and accolades that come with it. But usually, when we arrive, it doesn't look or feel quite how we imagined. Even if the success is not designed to be celebrated by others or a public affair, the internal success also doesn't marry with the one we had been visualising. We might not feel the way we anticipated or look the way we had expected, or even have a higher understanding after the journey itself.

The best way I can describe this outside of a business success, is when I became a father for the first time. I remember anticipating that I would feel like a parent and have the maturity and characteristics I had seen in my own mum and dad. But when my head hit the pillow at 3am after my wife had given birth to Oliver (of which she did a fantastic job), I just remember thinking I felt no different and that maybe it would come the following morning. Days of waiting turned to weeks and then months, and even though I loved and adored my new baby boy, that feeling of being a father never came. I felt like a missing jigsaw piece that was supposed to slot into this chapter of my life never materialised. What was even stranger was that the more I focused on it being missing, the bigger the hole became.

It was very similar when I was sat in The Cave. The success was anticlimactic, and I had expected this missing entrepreneurial jigsaw piece to have slotted into place, and it just didn't happen. I had visualised how it might look and feel, how it would connect with my current picture. But when I arrived at success, the void remained open, leaving the snapshot of where the picture was incomplete.

So what would any sane person do if they had completed a complex 10,000-piece jigsaw puzzle, got to the end, and realised there was a piece missing? The answer is exactly what most of us do in this situation: We start looking for it. The problem? The jigsaw we are talking about is in our mind and isn't a physical picture. It's the *feeling* of success that is missing. So, we start to search for that feeling anywhere we can find it, going to the low-hanging fruit first: dopamine hits.

Dopamine is our body's reward mechanism for a job well done and one place that has been honed to give it to us for little rewards is always readily available – our smartphones. Every notification we respond to, every like we receive on social media, every text, ding, and alert is a little to-do for our body to complete. Once done, it gives us that tiny hit of dopamine and success. This is why we find ourselves procrastinating with our phones so often. It is able to fill some of the void in the picture by giving us lots of tiny dopamine hits to remind us just how great we are, when the massive success we just achieved is missing its final jigsaw piece. Sometimes these moments of lacklustre feelings towards our achievements and our urge to search for the validations we thought would happen can last minutes. Other times they can span years, eating into our valuable creativity and ability to grow, all because a picture or feeling isn't quite what we expected it to be. Think back to a time when you have reached a great part of your life, only to start questioning an area of it that could be left alone.

How many times have you found pitfalls in the destination you have reached, which may or may not have resulted in you making changes to your environment to correct the areas it highlighted? For the vast majority, I would imagine something instantly popped into your mind. Your brain has already begun taking you down the road of validating the reasons you found the issues and the actions you took because of it.

How can we stop ourselves from searching for the missing pieces to our puzzles both in general life and business, so that when we reach our planned success, we can enjoy the view for as long as we choose? And if we want to, we size up the next summit? The answer is perspective: changing the way we enjoy our successes along the way.

How many times have you achieved success, only to crack straight on with the next task, not celebrating the journey you have just been on? For me, this happens all the time if I am not tuned into it. This is because I have a huge growth appetite. But what it also means is those little missing puzzle pieces start to mount up. Each time I reach the next level, that void seems even bigger.

This is the first thing I changed when I realised I was not enjoying the successes as they came. I was instead just getting my head down and moving onto the next one in the hopes that it would feel different. I now have regular moments planned in the diary where I can truly reflect and enjoy what the journey taught me, where it brought me to, and where it opened up my next door or path to follow. Sometimes, these are 15 minutes with a coffee, others they are holidays with family, others are QGMs and AGMs with my business teams. For you, they can be whatever you need them to be. Just make sure you spend time reflecting and reliving the moments that made the journey a success.

Once we learn to celebrate the successes we have made along the way, it will become very clear that the journey holds a ton more success, learning and happiness than the destination does. You are not going to arrive at the ticker tape parade, so you might as well focus on enjoying every day you are still working on your goals. Every day we get to wake up and work on our businesses, our passions and our relationships. It is a gift that is worth more than any accolade or destination. This is the first perspective shift we all need to make to ensure our journey to success is, well, successful. There is another perspective that also needs to change. If you focus on it enough, it can shorten the searching urges or completely remove them altogether.

The perspective shift I'm referring to is the missing jigsaw piece and how we need to change our view and relationship with it. For years, I viewed the missing piece of the jigsaw as a problem, a small piece of my mind that was missing and needed to be filled. It had always tarnished the successes regardless of their size. It left each picture incomplete, and I still had no idea of how to fill the void...until I shifted my perspective of how I viewed the void altogether. I had realised that the more I focused on it, the bigger the missing jigsaw piece became. I would then try to fill it with things that didn't fit its shape. On the other hand, if I tried to ignore the void, it left me feeling incomplete and the success I earned felt tarnished. So how could I solve the problem if I could neither focus on it nor ignore it? The answer lies in the way we view the void. For the rest of this chapter, I want to give you a practical way you can change your perspective of each void you discover, so that you can enjoy each success to the maximum.

To understand if you are at the point where this will work for you, ensure the answer to these questions are all a resounding "yes":

1. Have you recently achieved a goal that would occasion a celebration or cheer?

2. Was the result anticlimactic?

3. Have you found yourself searching for something to replace the feeling of success?

If the answers to the above three questions are yes, then the likelihood is you have a missing jigsaw piece. Below, I've listed a process that will help you overcome the feeling of a void, and replace it with the excitement to push onwards on your journey to success.

Enjoy the View

I want you to visualise a beautiful jigsaw in which the picture you are building is a moment in time that makes you happy and fills you with pride. It could be somewhere you have been before – whether it be a landscape, a family event or with friends. I want you to visualise the built jigsaw laid out in front of you. As you step back to admire the moment in time, you notice that there is one piece missing.

Front and Centre

Where have you pictured the piece is missing from? For me, it sits in the bottom right-hand corner, and yours might be somewhere else in the picture. It might be a significant piece of the picture or it might be a blotch of colour that makes up the background. Wherever you have viewed it is fine, but now we all need to move that missing piece, slap bang in the centre of the jigsaw, because we are about to change what the piece looks like.

The Window of Opportunity

A jigsaw piece has a number of grooves that either protrude from the piece or are indented, as they are designed to marry up to the pieces to the sides, above, and below, perfectly connecting together. What I want you to do with the void in your image is to smooth all sides of the void so that you are left with what looks like a traditional square or rectangle.

This is because to stop these feelings of loss or gaps in our successful moments, we need to stop thinking of them as missing pieces to the jigsaw, but instead see them as a window of opportunity.

The picture we have in our minds is the feeling we dreamed about when we were setting our goals. It is the force that has driven us to achieve them and reach success. We might have travelled months through rough terrain, crossing canyons and rivers before we had the opportunity to climb the summit and arrive at our completed goals. It leaves us looking at a breathtaking view. As we gaze out and enjoy the moment, the minute we begin to feel the missing parts that we were expecting, we need to bring into view the new window we have created, and step through it into the next part of our journey.

That missing jigsaw piece, that feeling of being incomplete, even when we are in a situation that should complete us, is not a void that needs to be filled. It is a gateway to the next stage of growth, and a natural part of our human desires. It will never be filled, because it stretches further than we can ever explore. Every new, completed journey will spark a new window of opportunity to explore. The perspective you need to take is that we are privileged to keep playing the game of life and live in a world where our hunger for growth is met with a never-ending buffet to eat from. It's not to be completed; it's to be enjoyed time and time again.

The next time you reach a goal or target, whether it is small or big, takes days or years – savour it and enjoy the view. Savour it because it feels great to enjoy it and because it's good to do so before checking out what lies past the next window of opportunity.

CHAPTER 13
STICKY TOFFEE PUDDING

Throughout the book, we have explored the past, planned the future and created the personal blueprint needed for your success. The strategies and learnings that have taken me a lifetime to realise and create are now yours to take forward to wherever your heart desires.

I would like to personally thank you for taking the time to read this book and congratulate you on doing the deep work. You have asked the difficult questions from your past and have taken the steps to plan and execute each and every part of the journey.

You might have noticed there is still one question left unanswered, which is: "What the hell has sticky toffee pudding got to do with your success?"

I saved this until the last chapter because to me it's as important, if not more so, than the rest of the book put together. This is Success Mindset 101 and without it, you're not going to enjoy the process nearly as much if you don't have your own sticky toffee pudding to walk away with. Don't worry, I've not lost the plot and there isn't a pudding on its way to you in the post. It's what the sticky toffee pudding represents that is important. In order for me to share that with you, I have one last story to tell.

I've shared a lot with you in this book about my childhood, my upbringing and different aspects of my success. They are all contributing factors to my success overall. So for our last lesson, we are going to focus on something that I have always battled with. It's something that, regardless of my success, has been a constant struggle for me: my relationship with food, my weight and my appearance overall.

This is something I inherited from the "Hill genes" in my family. If you speak to any of the males in my family, you will find that it is commonplace for them to have multiple different wardrobes at home, to house their fat, medium and thin clothes. We are a family of yo-yo dieters and growing up, I spent a fair amount of my youth avoiding the thin wardrobe altogether.

There has always been a running joke in our household about food, with my dad's famous line at the end of each meal being, "Well, it would be a shame to see it go to waste," as he would reach in for his third helping, much to my stepmom's disgust. If you're a Hill, you have two settings: "diet mode" where you are rigid and strict, or "off the wagon mode," where you could be a real danger to a company's profits at an all-you-can-eat buffet.

That's just how it's always been, and it took me a long time to realise why we did everything to the extreme and the damage it did to us in the long run. When I was in diet mode, my wife could never quite believe my resilience to temptation. How could I not have just one square of chocolate or that one bag of crisps? Whereas for me, it has always been all or nothing – the tap is either off or very much on!

This characteristic has its good sides, which include being able to switch off from anything that deviates from the path to success (in this case, the sat-nav destination being my thin wardrobe). But as we all know, every gift has its curse, and this instance is not an exception to the rule.

Much like in the Health, Wealth and Happiness Triangle, imagine the effort you put into anything being like pushing a pendulum in one direction. The harder and longer you swing it that way, the harder it's going to swing back! Which is why, after all the effort of being restrictive in my diet pays off and I can finally slip into those 28-inch jeans with ease, the reality is this: It won't be long until I'm hit with the backswing, and the inches will begin increasing with every buffet I visit!

The same can be said of success, which is where this story now becomes relevant to you. If you spend all of your time focusing on success, the pendulum will eventually have to course correct and you will find that all that momentum and success can be lost to self-sabotage. Your productivity will be shot, and you will make bad choices. You will have to hope and pray that you have done enough to stay afloat through the bad patches, so you can rebuild once the pendulum has balanced the books.

I realised that in dieting, success or anything that requires large volumes of effort, you always have to make sure it is sustainable, which in turn means not taking it too seriously. If you don't allow yourself to have a little fun along the way, you will end up in a bad place, and the time it would have taken to stop and smell the roses might be replaced with the need to replant the whole garden. You see this in business, in relationships, with athletes – anywhere passion takes hold: It removes any room to breathe and rest on the journey. This is where sticky toffee pudding comes in for me.

When I go on a dieting phase or fitness regime, or when I want to get just a little bit more in shape for a holiday, I allow myself to be strict day-to-day. But when I go to a restaurant, a friend's house or am eating out somewhere and there is a sticky toffee pudding on the menu, my non-negotiable is that, even if it will push me over my calories for the day or go against my target, I'm having that sticky toffee pudding! Success has to be sustainable, and for me the sticky toffee pudding rule keeps me from just focusing on success and pushing the pendulum in one direction. It helps me enjoy the journey for what it is.

The truth is, there's no pot of gold at the end of the rainbow. The "gold" is how what we are chasing shines bright, and we should enjoy every moment we experience along the way. Outside of our entrepreneurial journey to success, there should be things that are more important to us, things that we would give up the entire journey in a heartbeat for. One of our core values in all of the Lifestyle Entrepreneur businesses is "family first," because without them, what is the point?

For me, the sticky toffee pudding represents all of the great things in life. Whether we reach our goals or not, whether we are pushing hard and grinding every single day at the top or the bottom of the mountain, these things remind us that there is more to life than success. They remind us to not take life too seriously. It symbolises the need for us to put down the laptop sometimes and not feel guilty for it. To take that day off to enjoy time with family and friends. To enjoy time for ourselves selfishly when we just need a break. And to define ourselves more than just entrepreneurs who want to conquer the world (or the first mountain).

As a gift to you, as this book comes to a close, I have one last task for you to complete. Now that you are in control of sex and status, you've got your sat-nav pre-programmed and your evolution locked in, you have the right people around you to support your journey and you have the courage and insight to stop and smell the roses when the gaps in the jigsaw appear, the last thing you need to do is choose what your symbolic sticky toffee pudding is. Whatever you choose it to be, make sure it is something that you savour every moment of. Ensure that you never put it above your desire to succeed, as it will be the thing that keeps your pendulum from swinging too hard and knocking you off track entirely.

If, like me, you find that sticky toffee pudding turns out to be the right totem for you, I only ask that you enjoy the benefits it brings to your journey and the insanely luxurious and varied taste that await you with each sitting (because no sticky toffee pudding is ever the same). If you find a particularly good one that comes highly recommended, email me a picture with the details on where I can get my hands on it. Send it to STP@lifestyle-entrepreneur.co.uk, and I'll be sure to check it out.

You should now have everything you need for the onward journey to success, and all that remains is for you to put your time, energy and urgency into completing your levels of success and enjoying what comes with each. For those who want to take this to the next level and work alongside us in one of your communities or programs, please do reach out so we can see how we can support you.

Printed in Great Britain
by Amazon